Emotional
Competence

Emotional Competence

How Teachers Can Get Students to Learn EASIER and Faster

SELINA JACKSON, MA

FIRST EDITION
Emotional Competence: How Teachers Can Get Students to Learn Easier and Faster

Copyright © 2013 by Selina Jackson, MA.

Missing Piece Publications
340 E. First Street, #3297
Tustin, CA 92781
www.missingpiecepublications.com

Note: This publication contains the opinions and ideas of its author. It is intended to provide helpful and informative material on the subject matter covered. It is sold with the understanding that the author and publisher are not engaged in rendering professional services in the book. If the reader requires personal assistance or advice, a competent professional should be consulted. The author and publisher specifically disclaims any responsibility for any liability, loss, or risk, personal or otherwise, which is incurred as a consequence, directly or indirectly, of the use and application of any of the contents of this book.

Most Missing Piece books are available at special quantity discounts for bulk purchases for sales promotions, premiums, fundraising, or educational use. Special books or book excerpts can also be created to fit specific needs. For details, write: Special Markets, Missing Piece Publications, 340 E. 1st Street #3297, Tustin, CA 92781

EMOTIONAL COMPETENCE: How Teachers Can Get Students to Learn Easier and Faster/Selina Jackson, MA. -- 1st ed.

ISBN 978-0-9892325-2-4 - perfectbound
ISBN 978-0-9892325-3-1 - ePub

ACKNOWLEDGMENTS

Thanks to all of the educators that I have worked with over the years who helped spark the ideas. Their experience, feedback, and professional knowledge were invaluable.

Thanks to all the students who allowed me to experiment and explore the many ways to improve student learning and success. Their patience, cooperation, and most of all sense of humor helped keep us all among the sane.

Thanks to my editor and friend Karen Benson. Your excitement, belief, and suggestions for my book really made the positive difference.

FOREWORD

This book will entertain you, shock you, and enlighten you. That means reading it will be very profitable for you.

Interestingly, the BIG, important question a teacher can ask is: "Is teaching working for me?" Why? Because you are either getting the results and feelings you want, or you have been giving yourself reasons why you are not.

Actually, reasons are used as excuses, or as attempts to prove yourself right. While you are thinking about that, understand that you are either not enjoying teaching because you really don't want to teach, or you need some proven methods and techniques to make your teaching-experience easier, happier, and more fulfilling. That's what this book is about.

Unfortunately, your mind will make you resist these new, more successful techniques, because your mind likes you to do what is familiar, even when the familiar is not working very well. So move beyond that now, and open your mind to the many satisfying possibilities this book provides for you.

Happily, you are going to love how Selina informs you, challenges you, solves your problems, and enlightens you. You are going to love how she delights you with new, proven questions, suggestions, and powerful words you will find easy to use successfully. She doesn't leave you wondering how to apply what she teaches, because she is herself an excellent teacher. Enjoy!

Dr. Kembleton Wiggins
Doctor of Education
Former Professor of Psychology

Table *of* Contents

EMOTIONAL COMPETENCE:

How Teachers Can Get Students to Learn Easier and Faster

"WE CAN EASILY FORGIVE A CHILD WHO IS
AFRAID OF THE DARK; THE REAL TRAGEDY OF
LIFE IS WHEN MEN ARE AFRAID OF THE LIGHT."
—*Plato*

The information in this book will transform your teaching and bring you success and fulfillment. Reading it now will bring you an awareness and insight into human nature that will benefit you in other areas of your life. Your profession impacts other areas of life and other areas of life impact your profession.

The techniques in this book place powerful strategies in your hands. You have heard "practice makes perfect." Let's add to that, "practice makes permanent." The more comfortable and skilled you become at using the strategies, the more power they bring you. Bonus: You'll be surprised at their simplicity. You will enjoy them and the ease they bring to your teaching.

This book is based on principles of cognitive and social psychology. Research shows the importance of positive social interaction and the interdependence between intellectual growth and emotional development. (Hinton, et al.)

At a time when classroom management and instruction strategies are failing and teachers who expected professional success are finding misery, you will be given tools to help you get what you want from your students. You will find *Emotional Competence: How Teachers Can Get Students to Learn Easier and Faster* a valuable contribution to your effectiveness in the classroom.

A new, exciting experience begins now. Are you ready to learn? Move forward.

PART ONE

The Role of Emotion in Teaching

"THE SECRET OF CHANGE IS TO FOCUS ALL OF
YOUR ENERGY, NOT ON FIGHTING THE OLD, BUT
ON BUILDING THE NEW."

—*Socrates*

H ave you ever wondered why you do things you don't want to do? Why you do things you promise you won't do? Why in spite of all you do, you're not as successful, fulfilled, and happy as you want to be? The secret lies in your subconscious mind.

Unchanneled, the subconscious puts a limit on your success in career, money, love, and health. When you get close to what you want, you begin to feel uncomfortable. You sabotage yourself. Lottery winners are a good example of this principle: they win millions and in a short time, most are broke again, many of them heavily in debt and fleeing unhappy relatives who didn't cash in to the tune they thought they would.

Mindset, more than circumstances or luck, determines success.

How Your Mind Works

I really like chocolate. If you like it, your subconscious likes it. If you say, "From now on I'm not going to eat any more chocolate," your subconscious falls down laughing and you continue your tawdry threesome with Mr. Hershey and Lady Godiva.

Here's how it works: Your conscious mind handles conscious thought. The subconscious, 70,000 times more powerful than the conscious, handles automatic responses (heart rate, blood pressure, breathing, instinct, etc.). It controls decision-making, motivation strategies, belief and emotional systems, and the forgotten decisions and beliefs of early childhood. In a conflict between conscious and subconscious, *the subconscious always wins*.

Negative beliefs and emotion connected with school will sabotage your success. Example: you have an opportunity to advance to an administrator position; your subconscious believes you don't deserve it. You will find yourself at the beach (naked as a jaybird) while Channel Five is doing a documentary on beached whales, and miss an important staff meeting because you are out buying up all the newspapers with photos of you on the front page holding both hands over your privates.

Ridding yourself of negative emotion empowers you to achieve the joy, fulfillment, and happiness available to you.

Part One of this book teaches you to do this with ease, speed, and certainty.

HOW TO EASILY APPLY IT

1. Your subconscious is there to protect you. Thank your subconscious for this.

2. In a conflict between your two minds, the subconscious ALWAYS wins. Get your subconscious on board with your conscious goals and desires.

3. When you're not in control, the subconscious is. Don't reprimand yourself. Realize that your subconscious is

(unsuccessfully) trying to help you. Example: screaming at your students doesn't work. Ask yourself, *what do I hope to accomplish by yelling and how can I effectively handle the class and get what I want?*

4. Discover your negative beliefs and limiting emotions about teaching and get rid of them. (So you don't end up in Malibu flashing your garbanzos.) Develop positive beliefs about yourself. You are about to learn how to do this.

CHAPTER ONE

Emotional Competence

"EMOTIONS NEED TO BE CONNECTED WITH THE INTELLECT. WHEN THE ANALYTICAL MIND IS ENGAGED WITH EMOTIONS AND INTUITION, YOUR SENSES AND EMOTIONAL INTELLIGENCE CAN SCAN IN MOMENTS THROUGH HUNDREDS OF POSSIBLE CHOICES OR SCENARIOS TO ARRIVE AT AN OPTIMUM SOLUTION IN A MATTER OF SECONDS."

—Cooper

EMOTIONAL COMPETENCE is a high level of skill in managing your and others' emotions to get the results you want. High skill means:

- You are aware of your emotional state at any given moment. You understand the hidden message each emotion produces and act accordingly.
- If you don't like the way you feel you instantly change it.
- You manage the mental state of others with ease, speed, and certainty. A student in an unproductive frame of mind will neither work nor be motivated to do well. You need to know how to help him.

Man, like every other species, is an emotional animal. Our feelings interfere with our desires. Understanding them helps us better serve our goals and purposes.

In this chapter you will discover:

- How to understand your Emotional Messaging System
- Ways to handle inconsideration, disrespect, and other rude, negative, and annoying behaviors
- The source of emotion
- How to easily shift into a positive frame of mind

The Meaning Of Emotion

1. Anxiety – inner conflict or negative expectations
2. Anger - reaction to violation of your values
3. Disappointment - a forerunner to giving up
4. Fear - perception of danger
5. Frustration - an obstacle between you and a goal
6. Hurt - recognition of ill-treatment at someone else's hands
7. Loneliness - a sense of unwanted isolation
8. Sadness- a sense of loss

Your Emotional Messaging System

It's natural to feel frustrated at times. Especially when the student who stole the Oscar three years in a row for his uncharted role of proverbial pimple on the nose of your most promising lesson plans shows up *again* this year.

Emotion is our messaging system. It lets us know what is happening, alerts us to danger; it is crucial to correctly interpret messages.

People mistake frustration for anger and vice versa, deceiving the subconscious. Frustration signals a block to a goal. If you interpret this as anger, your subconscious will respond in anger, leading to problems.

A history teacher struggled to get through his lesson. The phone rang. Someone came into the room with a note from the office. The phone rang again. The attendance monitor came to pick up his sheet and the teacher had to take roll. There was a fire drill. This went on until there were only fifteen minutes left in the period.

Class resumed and kids in the back of the room started talking. The teacher went off.

He yelled, "Derwood, I'm sick and tired of you talking. You know you're not supposed to do that! You're wasting our time. We can't even get through the review. You're getting a referral! Get out NOW!"

"That's not fair! I didn't do anything!" Derwood yelled back.

The teacher countered, "I don't care. I'm sick of dealing with this. You're suspended. Now get out of here!"

Derwood banged his desk as he rose, hurled a book to the floor, and his middle finger sprang to attention. "Screw you!" He glared at the teacher for a long tense moment before storming out, slamming the door.

What happened? This teacher was frustrated. Circumstances blocked him from his goal. He told himself he was angry and his subconscious took over. Naturally Derwood's behavior reflected the teacher's mood. Richard Restack, MD, author of *The New Brain*, says, "Anger and resentment are the most contagious of all emotions." If the teacher had recognized his frustration, he would have responded to Derwood differently and avoided unnecessary anguish.

It's been said that we have more words to label others than we have to label our feelings. (Rosenberg) Understanding emotional messages is the first step to a higher level of communication.

As infants we expressed ourselves without inhibition. As we grew we were trained to distrust and evade our feelings.

The question is, what do you do with them? If you're like most people, what you didn't learn to do with your emotions as a child is causing you unnecessary unhappiness.

What People Don't Learn

The ability to express emotion comes from childhood modeling. Example: a child throws a tantrum and gets slapped. He is told, "Shut up. Stop crying. Why are you acting that way?" His subconscious connects anger to punishment.

CHILDREN SHOULD BE SEEN AND NOT HEARD

 Children have traditionally been stifled: nice people don't get angry. It is not okay to cry in public. Don't yell, it isn't nice. Don't be mad, don't be sad. Never make a scene in public. We must behave in a seemly manner.

"The silencing of feelings is a tragic issue in many families." (Hawkins [David, not Sadie])

You swallow pain and anger to protect you from the unpleasant result of expressing yourself.

Your anger stays inside, eats at you and eventually explodes. Stress causes heart attacks, strokes, cancer, intestinal diseases and other serious health issues.

THE ABILITY TO EXPRESS NEGATIVE EMOTION IN A POSITIVE WAY is the beginning of healthy communication and emotional competence.

Recognize the messages of the heart. This book will teach you to express them in a meaningful way and let them go. Denying and swallowing pain does not rid you of them; buried emotions do not die. They fester and erupt. "The benefits of strengthening our feelings vocabulary are evident not only in intimate relationships, but also in the professional world." (Hawkins)

The Five Basic Rights — Developed by Karen Benson

In the course of human events, humans offend one another, often by accident. The resultant pain, fear, and anger have to be dealt with in healthy ways that create a win-win situation and release negativity from the victim whose rights have been envicted. From birth to death we are endowed with certain human rights, all God given and many protected by civil law. The following is an explanation and description of those rights.

1. Your person, or physical self. You have the right not to be hit, kicked, pinched, bitten, or any other form of physical abuse. You also have the right not to be physically invaded by any act of unwelcome affection--touching, patting, kissing, hugging, rubbing, etc.

2. Your property. Nobody has the right to steal, damage, destroy, or borrow without returning anything that belongs to you.

3. Your privacy. Your personal life is your own. Nobody has the right to peek through your windows, go through your mail, or betray your confidence. Questions about your weight, your age, your finances, or your love life, if they render you uncomfortable, are invasions of your privacy.

4. Free agency, or freedom of choice. You have the right to make your own choices, your own decisions, and your own mistakes. Parents have the right to protect young children from danger. As children grow, their right of choice becomes greater, and parents have no right to interfere with the decisions and choices of their adult offspring.

5. Your feelings. Any communication with the word *you* followed by a negative message invades your feelings. Any message, verbal or non-verbal, that leaves you feeling diminished, embarrassed, rejected, angry, fearful, worthless (the list goes on), is an emotional offense. So are sarcasm, yelling, and threats.

There are four responses to the aggression that violates these rights.

1. React to the offender by invading his rights (name-calling, blaming, insulting, hitting back, etc) (aggressive, unhealthy).

2. Absorb the hurt and say nothing (passive, unhealthy).

3. Absorb the hurt and get even later by sabotage (passive-aggressive, unhealthy).

4. Express how you feel and ask for what you want (assertive, healthy).

Assertiveness is sometimes mistaken for aggression. It isn't. The word *assert* means to step forth to claim a right. Aggression invades the rights of others, passivity allows aggression, and assertiveness is a state of respect for the rights of others and healthy responses when offenses occur. Your role as a teacher is to teach students about the roles and model healthy expression of emotion for your students.

Aggressive People

+ Take what they want at the expense of the rights of others

+ Are bullies and abusers

+ Use fear and intimidation as weapons

+ Instill anxiety in others

+ Are easy to respect (it's hard not to be extremely deferential to a guy who is chasing you with a pick axe) and very difficult to love

Passive People

+ Say yes when they want to say no

- Are willing victims who allow others to violate their rights

- Are silent and fearful

- Stuff down pain, fear, and anger until they erupt

- Make excuses for their abusers ("It's my fault he hit me, I made him mad----")

- Are easy to love and very difficult to respect

Passive-Aggressive People

- Seethe inside instead of speaking up

- Will get you later (sabotage) in ways that have nothing to do with what offended them

The respect aggressors receive is based on fear, which eventually becomes hatred and resentment. The love passive people receive is based on pity, which ultimately becomes contempt.

Assertive People

- Freely express their desires and feelings

- Neither abuse nor allow themselves to be abused

- Attain both love and respect

- Excel in qualities of self-esteem and courage, which assertiveness establishes and promotes

- Are a safe receptacle for your feelings

Assertiveness is achieved in two simple steps:

1. Say how you feel.

2. Ask for what you want.

The word *simple* is used here instead of easy because assertiveness seems strange and unnatural when we handle our emotions in a less than healthy way. If you find yourself in an unhealthy area, it's okay. We lack assertiveness because nobody ever taught it to us. To attain it, all you have to do is *consistently* ask for what you want and express how you feel. This behavior engenders assertiveness in others and establishes and maintains the dignity and self-esteem of us and the people we communicate with.

Here are some examples:

- *I feel angry because my professional time was not respected*

- *When I lose an opportunity I deserve for extra paid duty, I feel deprived*

- How much did you get paid for tutoring after school? *I don't feel comfortable talking about money.*

- Mrs. Jones, you're old and crabby and you need to retire. *Freddy, I don't like it when you say negative things to me, and I want you to be on your best behavior in the classroom.*

- *I feel hurt and embarrassed when you circulate copies of my mug shot*

Compromise, negotiate, and listen. Examples:

- *I don't want to be in charge of this. What do you think?*
- *We have different ideas on this project. How can we both get what we want?*
- *I like your idea, but I want to add to it. Can we work together on this?*
- *

ALWAYS EXPRESS POSITIVE FEELINGS. Examples:

- *I feel encouraged when you point out what I am doing that is working*
- *I like hearing that*
- *I appreciate you helping to make our classroom run smoothly*
- *Thank you for getting Willoughby to do his homework*

"Because we spend much of our lives at work, and it's the place that potentially offers us confidence and satisfaction, healthy relationships at work are not optional--they are imperative." (Hawkins again)

In Your Experience

On the assertiveness scale, what role do you play in the classroom?

_____

_____

_____

Is it working for you? If not, are you willing to follow the simple above steps to healthy behavior? Are you willing to teach your children by precept and example to express their feelings and ask for what they want?

I know you are. Congratulations.

The Source of Human Feeling

What makes people feel the way they feel? Example: tomorrow your neighbor is giving a garden party she's planned for weeks. You decide to paint your house. You wake up and it's raining. You say, "Well, I can put off that paint job and relax today." Your neighbor thinks, "Darn, there goes my party." She is disappointed. You are relieved.

The rain did not bring your disappointment, your reaction did.

Example: Sophronia enters the room, nostrils flaring, and bellows "Heeey!" in a voice that would send Fran the Nanny Drescher running for earplugs. Your students, happy for the diversion because they weren't listening anyway, start laughing and talking, behavior you interpret as a hostile takeover.

It's not Sophronia's behavior that makes you cringe, it's your evaluation of that behavior. (Which wasn't really a hostile takeover, she was just recovering from a run-in with the West Side Flasher.)

Change what you believe and you change the way you feel. "There is a critical link between emotion and our perceptions of events." (Lazarus [not the one from the Bible])

The Self-Fulfilling Belief System

This shocking true story demonstrates just how powerful beliefs can be.

> A man worked for a shipping company. His job was to take care of the refrigerator car. One day as he stacked crates in a corner, the door closed and jammed. He banged on it and yelled for help. No one heard him. The next morning he was dead. The autopsy revealed he had frozen to death. When they checked the car the refrigeration wasn't on. The man froze to death because he believed he would.

Consider these facts:

1. We create what we believe.
2. People treat us the way we believe they will.
3. Our problems are a result of what we tell ourselves.

Your circumstances are created by your beliefs. If you have difficulty getting what you want, you believe life is difficult.

Beliefs direct the way we think, feel, and behave. Limiting beliefs keep us from recognizing prospects. If you believe "I never win," circumstances will decree that you never win.

Remember that time George Clooney proposed marriage to you? And Bill Gates gave you that big story about investing in some computer stock? And you men remember when Madonna told you she'd do just anything in the world for a ride in your car? When these opportunities arose you weren't interested because you were putting your money in a Christmas Club account, didn't want Madonna to screw up your relationship with your girlfriend Rosie O'Donnell, and you knew Bill Gates was a phony from the word go.

One who believes "I deserve to be successful" looks for ways to turn failure into triumph. Positive beliefs allow us to see what helps us reach our goals.

Many of our beliefs came from parents, teachers, peers, the media. If I showed you a pen and told you it was a lollipop, you'd wonder where I got my degrees. You already know what a lollipop is (critical factor). Before the age of four (and sometimes up until seven), there is no critical factor. Everything children see, hear, feel goes directly into the subconscious mind as true. Without critical evaluation we believe everything.

What the subconscious mind doesn't agree with it rejects. If you believe you're ugly, no amount of industrial strength Estee Lauder will make you feel presentable and there is not a potato big enough to make you feel good in your swim shorts.

If you feel inadequate in a classroom, no amount of professional development will put you in control of your class. The best kids in the world will have you tied to a chair and set on fire by recess.

A mismatch between your beliefs and your desires creates anxiety. Fear and doubt take over your ability to think rationally. You miss out on the happiness available to you.

Any negative thought (or word) creates tension. "Chronic stress is a very real issue at schools for both staff and students ." (Jenson, et. al.)

Examine your beliefs about yourself and what is possible. Make sure your beliefs match the results you want. This next exercise will help.

In Your Experience — *Complete these statements with the first thing that comes to mind.*

1. What makes it impossible for me to do well professionally is...

2. If there were an emotional reason for not doing well, it would be...

3. If I did well the consequences would be...

4. In order to do well I have to...

5. Instead of success, I really want...

6. What hangups do I have about doing well?

Check your answers for limiting beliefs. Let them go. Choose empowering ones.

How to Easily Shift into a Positive Frame of Mind

Positive teaching mode is crucial for you and your students. If you feel anger or frustration, you'll sabotage your success. Here's how.

Your frontal lobe enables you to exercise judgment and make good decisions. In times of emotional upheaval the lobe shuts down; blood goes into your limbic system to deal with emotion. You respond to situations and people through your emotional brain. Example: at break time, you lock yourself in the ladies room, light up, take a drag, deeply inhale before realizing you're in the janitor's closet.

Avoiding this requires the ability to leave personal issues at home. Here's how: Say *"I choose to remember that school is not home."* The mind immediately separates the two, allowing you to fully engage your professional self.

Questioning Strategy works because the mind cannot NOT answer a question. If I asked you, "Where were you this time yesterday?" your brain would find an answer.

A question about a past experience forces you to re-experience it consciously and subconsciously. A question regarding mood will cause you to experience that mood. The following question will put you in positive teaching mode: *What would it be like if I were in a positive teaching frame of mind now?*

Your mind will respond and you will experience the frame of mind in question.

NOTE: You will achieve the desired frame of mind if you are clear about what is is. Ask yourself: What response do I want? And what frame of mind do I need for a natural response? Put yourself in that mode and take control of your day.

HOW TO EASILY APPLY IT

1. Improve your ability to handle yourself emotionally. Get in the habit of asking yourself, "How do I feel about this?" If you don't like the answer, attain a more positive feeling.

2. Avoid misinterpreting your emotions (calling frustration anger and vice versa). Frustration, not anger, signifies a block between you and your goal.

3. Express yourself assertively: Say how you feel and ask for what you want.

4. Let go of limiting beliefs. Choose beliefs that match desired results. Example: you doubt your ability to get classroom cooperation. Choose to believe you *will* get it. Behave as if it is true. You will be pleasantly surprised at the results.

5. ALWAYS be in positive teaching mode before you enter the classroom. Ask yourself: *How would I know if I were in a positive frame of mind right now? What would it be like?* These two questions make attainment of this principle powerful. And your mind puts you there. Easy.

CHAPTER TWO

Designing Your Day for Optimal Results

> "OBSTACLES ARE THOSE FRIGHTFUL THINGS YOU SEE WHEN YOU TAKE YOUR EYES OFF YOUR GOAL."
> —*Henry Ford*

Research reveals that teacher quality is the most crucial factor in student success. The quality of your teaching is directly related to your ability to plan and present learning opportunities.

We all know lesson planning is part of good teaching. It includes what you want students to learn, the parts of the lesson (*I do, we do, and you do*), and other data. Why don't all teachers plan consistently? Lack of time and a sense of being overwhelmed are the most common responses.

Duties seem neverending: keeping up with the pacing guide; grading and report cards; discipline; tasks assigned by administration. The ability to get it all done is attained by management of subconscious priorities.

In this chapter you will discover:

- How to manage subconscious priorities
- How to avoid being a victim of circumstance
- Examples of Positive Outcome Statements

Managing Subconscious Priorities

Your mind organizes tasks into a hierarchy of importance. No two things occupy the same space, no two tasks have the same priority. To not know that is to be overwhelmed. A teacher wished to spend more time with her family, but stayed late at school during the week. On weekends she caught up on school business. Consciously her family was most important; her subconscious had another priority.

Here's how to get what you want:

- List tasks
- Prioritize the list. If something low on the list matters most, rearrange the list
- Begin with what is most important

This empowers you to get it done with ease and comfort.

Avoid Being a Victim of Circumstance

Have you ever watched a wonderful lesson go south? Determine how your day will go. Example: *I intend to enjoy teaching today.*

Many people suffer needlessly because they haven't made a distinction between *what happened* vs. *what do I want.* They get stuck on the negative events: *Stanley Awfulheimer just won't pay attention, that darned office intercom is always interrupting my lesson, those uncaring parents never support my efforts.* Rehearsing what happened will bring you more of that negativity. Ask: *what do I want instead?* Give your brain a goal to get it.

A well-formed goal puts you in total control. Example: *I intend to handle interruptions with comfort and ease. I've decided to teach with patience, confidence, and enthusiasm.*

Do you want to teach this way? Announce your intention to do so. Do you want to feel satisfied at the end of the day? Write that goal. Experiencing day-to-day activities (instructional periods, phone calls, meetings) without a clear outcome in mind sets you up for ineffectiveness.

Intention measures emotion and behavior. Your brain is a goal-seeking mechanism, geared for achievement. Without a present goal, it will seek one from your (negative) past.

Example: an unmotivated student gave you trouble. He talked while you talked, distracted others from learning, and was disrespectful and defiant. You ended up frustrated and angry. Your present students talk while you talk. If you don't set an intention to stop to it, your brain will trigger the pain caused by your past student. You become a victim of circumstance, of unhealthy emotion, of other people's behavior.

"Specific goals lead to higher performance, increase focus, minimize distractions, provide energy for the task." (Locke and Latham, et. al.) Decide *exactly* what you want. Don't leave anything to chance or to feelings of the  moment; you'll attract more of what you don't want. If you feel negative ask yourself, "*What do I want to feel instead?*" Set a goal for that feeling. "*I allow myself to feel calm and confident during transitions.*" Or ask yourself, "*What outcome do I want as a result of this transaction?*" Then create a positive outcome statement.

Examples of Powerful Positive Outcome Statements

- *I've decided that at the end of the day I will be satisfied that I have done my best*
- *I intend that I teach today as comfortably, easily, and effectively as possible*
- *I choose to make the most of myself and my abilities today*

"People waste time and energy trying to control others, disbelieving they can change their own thoughts and feelings." (Ellis and Harper) How much happier and more fulfilled would you like to feel in your professional life? You can have more beneficial outcomes when you set your goals ahead of time.

In Your Experience — *Before teaching each day, be very clear about what you want. People don't get what they want by running from what they don't want: that creates a vacuum. (The mind doesn't like empty space, it will fill it.)* Answering these questions can help. Then write a positive outcome statement (POS) for each answer.

1. What kind of energy do I want to experience when I teach?

   _____

   POS - _____

   _____

2. How do I wish to feel as a result of my efforts at the end of the day?

   _____

   POS - _____

   _____

3. How do I wish to handle interruptions?

   _____

   POS - _____

   _____

   Clarifying this means you've given your brain the go-ahead to achieve it.

HOW TO EASILY APPLY IT

1. ALWAYS plan your lessons.

2. Manage your subconscious priorities to avoid being overwhelmed.

3. Design your day. Decide exactly what

outcomes you want ahead of time and write a Positive Outcome Statement. People who write their goals achieve them faster and easier.

CHAPTER THREE

The Power of Your Words

"DEATH AND LIFE IS IN THE POWER OF THE TONGUE."

—*King Solomon*

Many people have talked themselves out of what they want. We speak through our thoughts. Psychologists call this self-talk. Did you know that we self-speak between 500 and 1500 words per minute? You do it so often you don't pay attention to it. Your subconscious does. It hears your thoughts and takes them literally, which is why you catch yourself driving by your ignorant, arrogant brother-in-law's house in Beverly Hills and throwing a bag of sour grapes at his Cadillac.

In this chapter we will discuss:

1. The Law of Suggestion
2. The low stress way to handle mistakes
3. Some harmful questions to avoid
4. How to counteract other people's negativity

The Law of Suggestion

Self-talk is actually self-hypnosis. A client told me why she had remained stuck for so long before seeking help. "That's how messed up I am." She laughed. Consciously we both understood that she was "just playing." On the subconscious level the meaning was clear: *since you've schmucked up your life big time, let me bring it to your attention so you can feel even worse about yourself than you already do.* No wonder she had procrastinated and self-sabotaged.

Your words contain power. They propel your subconscious into action. How can simple words produce such enormous results? If you make statements like:

I'm broke.
This job sucks.
I'll never get a master's degree.
I'm too old to go back to school.
I'm too tired to learn anything.
My marriage will never work out.

These statements, even in fun, create negative vibes, which attract more negativity to you. This is the Law of Suggestion.

Try this interesting experiment. Read the following question or statement and pay attention to what happens in your mind.

- Why are you suddenly thinking of someone you haven't thought of in a very long time?
- Don't think of the answer to 2 + 2 now.
- Don't think about a problem you're dealing with.

What did you notice? Did you find yourself thinking *exactly* what the statement or question told you to ignore?

Are you sentencing yourself to hard time with your words? People cause themselves unnecessary health problems through negative verbiage. Every cell in the body has intelligence and responds to words. Example: you just bought new jeans. You try them on, look in the mirror, frown and say, "I don't like my butt." Guess what? Your butt hears you and says, "Well, frankly my dear, I'm not all that crazy about you either." Your behind is now the size of Montana. "Your body reacts to your every thought as the limbic system translates your emotional state into physical sensations of relaxation or tension." (Amen)

Society teaches us to focus on what we don't want. It has trained us to beat ourselves up in order to make progress. When a child brings home a "D," his parents scold him, thinking they are motivating him to do better. They are actually training their child to chastise himself in order to improve. The child develops self-sabotaging behaviors that make it hard to control his negativity. "We can select a more optimistic response." (Restak)

The Low Stress Way to Handle Mistakes

In achieving goals you're going to make mistakes along the way. It's inevitable; you're human. If you have to always be flawless and perform perfectly, your subconscious will not allow you to make mistakes without punishing yourself. This belief stops you from learning and growing; we *have* to make mistakes in order to learn.

Did you know that airplanes fly off course more than 90% of the time? Crosswinds take over. How do they arrive at their destination? They have built-in self-correcting instruments. So do you.

When we apply negative labels to adverse circumstances we create stress. Example: you step in a large specimen straight from a dog's lower digestive tract on your way to a formal dinner. Cursing dogs in general and St. Bernards in particular is going to make for a very unhappy evening. Cursing your date for not seeing it before you stepped in it is also not productive. "Adopting an optimistic explanation of things is more healthy, more motivating and is more associated with success." (Seligman)

Telling yourself that the large jumbo canine in question was unable to find a public toilet and is therefore blameless will make you feel much better.

The happiest people are dedicated to a positive outlook and never-ending improvement. They see mistakes as learning opportunities. You can too. Decide now to ask yourself: *What valuable lesson can (did) I learn from this?*

Harmful Questions to Avoid

When things don't go as planned, people beat themselves up. They berate themselves with reprimands like "I should have known better." They ask negative questions:

What's wrong with me?
Why can't I get this right?
Am I an idiot or what?

This causes even more problems because of the *search factor* in your mind. Negative questions send your mind on a quest for answers. The result is the misery that accompanies negative self-information. Emotion determines behavior, so you find yourself reacting badly in the form of sticking pins in your own hex doll, making crank calls to the superintendent of schools, and putting gum on the seats in your students' parents' SUVs.

When our goals and values are compromised, we choose one of two approaches: demand that adversity not happen or accept setbacks and find solutions. Ask questions that yield results you want. Example:

How do I know when things are going well?
Why is it easy for me to get this right?
How come I'm feeling so confident about finding a solution?
How can I refuse to let the bowel problems of a St. Bernard ruin my evening?

With practice, positive answers will come automatically when you need them.

Counteract Other Peoples' Negativity

You've decided to be a positive influence in your school. You're happily walking towards your room when you catch a glimpse of Martha Miserable. You look around for a fast escape. Too late. She spots you and waves you over. As usual she looks like she suffers from painful hemorrhoids. You discover you are beginning to feel her pain, which makes you rather nervous.

Did you know that when you're within three feet of negaholics you breathe in their vibes? This results in tension headache, exacerbation of that pesky tic in your right eye, and gastric disruptions usually associated with being kicked in the gut by a bad-tempered mule.

What can you do? Think: *Love.* (Yes, really.)

Love is the most powerful force in the universe. Example: I booked a flight and decided to change it. The airline charged a $100 fee. I explained my situation to an agent and asked that the fee be waived. She told me no, then asked me to hold after I threatened to destroy her family. As I waited I thought, *"Love is good."* After a few minutes, she returned and said, "We don't normally do this, but we will waive the fee."

Try love and watch what happens.

Empower yourself to counteract other people's low energy words. Example: in the lunch room you accidentally overhear a teacher threaten to destroy somebody's family. (She must deal with my airline.)

How do you protect yourself from the painful results of accidentally overhearing other people's conversations? When you desire to negate the negative, say "I cancel that." If you say it within fourteen seconds you keep it from entering your subconscious and affecting you. The beauty of this is you don't have to say it aloud. Amazing.

It works even better when you improve your ability to handle stressful people and situations. Example: you overhear your neighbor saying to her mother on the phone (you overhear this because you have your phone line hooked up to their house), "That Jackson woman next door is a pain in the behind." You immediately say, "I cancel that," which is a lot better than going over and torching her garage. You say "I reject that," several times, then, just because you're such a good neighbor, you lock your blow torch in the tool shed and hide the key.

HOW TO EASILY APPLY IT

1. Use the Law of Suggestion in your favor: speak what you want rather than what you have.

2. Choose to believe in constant improvement; you'll do better and feel happier.

3. Avoid negative questions which will instruct your mind to supply painful answers. Ask questions that achieve results you want.

4. When you're within three feet of someone, take control of how you feel: think loving thoughts.

5. Protect yourself from the unhappy results of other people's negativity. Cancel or reject it. Improve your ability to handle stressful people and situations. Say: *I choose to believe consciously and subconsciously that I handle stressful situations and stressful people better and better every day. And I'm glad I chose that belief.*

6. Congratulate yourself, you're on your way to a mindset that will bring you joy, peace, and harmony with the people around you.

CHAPTER FOUR

Discovering Your Core Purpose

"HE WHO HAS A WHY TO LIVE FOR CAN BEAR
ALMOST ANY HOW."
—*Nietzsche*

Know thyself. Internal authenticity is vital to our emotional, spiritual, social, and intellectual development. Failure to know oneself is to:

- Live with goals set by other people
- Marry the wrong person
- Settle for an unacceptable job
- Lack awareness of one's own feelings and beliefs

To know yourself is to set yourself up for success in your work, in your life, in your business dealings, in relationships.

In this chapter you will discover:

1. Your core values in terms of teaching
2. The proper alignment of your teaching goals with your purpose
3. Designer exercises that help create your best school life

Your Core Values

It is not enough to just plan lessons and set goals. The question is, "What do you want to accomplish through your teaching?" This is about your purpose—seeing beyond tasks to the powerful influence you have on the lives and futures of your students.

If you teach solely to make a living, you'll never experience the joy and fulfillment available to you. If you are teaching because you believe you're supposed to, you're living someone else's goal, not your own. The painful result is frustration, unhappiness, needless stress.

The key is to find your own professional fulfillment. This journey starts by exploring those dreams. Viable goals are a subset of life purpose and are always about the heart. What you get doesn't appear through conscious decision; it appears through your heart's desires.

A client said she married her husband "because I felt safe in his arms." That's the heart. Unless you get excited about a goal, it's not *your* goal.

How did you get into teaching? What made you choose it? Does it excite you? If not, you might be in it for the wrong reason. If you have to take five happy pills to get out of bed on school days, there is most likely some hidden conflict that must be eliminated.

The following exercise will help you become aware of the alignment (or lack of) between your purpose and your teaching goals. The closer your goals are aligned to your purpose, the more clear, compelling and easier they are to achieve.

In Your Experience

1. Why do I teach? (This is about YOU.)

_____

_____

_____

2. What about teaching gives me the greatest feeling of importance?

_____

_____

_____

3. As a teacher, what do I care about most deeply? How do I want to be remembered?

_____

_____

_____

4. What am I most professionally committed to?

_____

_____

_____

5. As a teacher, what do I *not* want?

_____

_____

_____

6. What action will ensure I remain true to my purpose?

_____

_____

Now you know what values are most important to you. Before you say YES or NO to a question, ask: *Will this get me closer or take me further from living my values and purpose?*

HOW TO EASILY APPLY IT

1. Know yourself.
2. Make sure your actions are in alignment with your values.
3. Remember the big picture—*your* legacy (and the accompanying fulfillment, happiness, and satisfaction).

CHAPTER FIVE

Designer Exercises for Creating Your BEST School Life

Congratulations. I believe you are reading this book because you want to be more than "just okay" in your career. I hope your desire is to be a great educator whose legacy will survive you for generations to come. This chapter will help you to become that outstanding teacher you want to be.

Imagine the emotional freedom and professional fulfillment you want. Imagine the happiest moments of your career. Because I want this for you I've included some powerful exercises. Don't try to do them all at once. These strategies are designed to help you shift at your core:

Exercise #1 - Optimizing Your Professional Role

Exercise #2 - Maximizing Your Emotional Competence

Exercise #3 - Best Solutions to Everyday Challenges

Exercise #4 - Optimizing Your Health

Allow yourself to accomplish the above in a way that is right for you so you can be delightfully surprised at the amazing results.

EXERCISE # 1 – Optimizing Your Role in Your Career

How would you like to have the ultimate teaching experience this year? Imagine how much more successful, deeply fulfilled, and happier you would be. This exercise is designed to help you.

PART ONE: Optimizing Your Role

1. What are my strengths and potential as a teacher?

   _____

   _____

   _____

2. How can I maximize them?

   _____

   _____

   _____

3. What are my weaknesses and liabilities?

   _____

   _____

   _____

4. What is the best way to minimize them?

   _____

   _____

   _____

5. How do I know when I am operating from my best self?

_____

_____

_____

6. How can I be my best self in every circumstance?

_____

_____

_____

7. How can I bring out the best in others?

_____

_____

_____

8. How can I insure that all communication results in a win-win?

_____

_____

_____

♥ Choose to be your best career self. This will produce optimum results. Get your subconscious on board with your desired results. Say:
  - *I've decided to be the best I can be in every circumstance from now on. And I release from my mind every thought to the contrary*
  - *I choose to forgive myself for past mistakes and dedicate myself to working at optimal level*
  - *I intend to bring out the best in others at all times and with ease*

EXERCISE #2 - Maximizing Your Emotional Competence

Your emotions are knocking on the door of your awareness. Are you at home? Ignoring or devaluing your feelings creates denial, frustration, and stress. Emotional pain signals a mismatch between your thoughts and actions and your highest self.

Even if you are emotionally in a good place, you have to deal with the emotions of others, including neurotics, negaholics, and students who are running on hormones and confusion. These powerful questions will help you meet your own emotional needs and the needs of people around you that you are forced by the cruel hand of fate to deal with.

1. What is the most effective way to increase my awareness and acceptance of my feelings?

   _____

   _____

   _____

2. What will I do to put myself into positive mode before I begin to teach?

   _____

   _____

   _____

3. How can I restore positive interaction in an emotionally upsetting situation?

   _____

   _____

   _____

4. What emotions are blocking me from the most enjoyable teaching experiences possible? What is the wisest way to resolve them?

_____

_____

_____

5. What is my most empowering emotion as a teacher? How can I maximize it?

_____

_____

_____

6. What is the most productive way to handle my students' emotional turmoil?

_____

_____

_____

7. The wisest way to increase my emotional wealth is by expressing gratitude. What three things am I most grateful for? How can I remind myself to express gratitude every day?

_____

_____

_____

8. There is a chemical called dopamine that makes learning (scratch that; it makes *everything*) easier. It spills into the brain when you're having fun. How can you tap into your sense of humor each day?

_____

_____

_____

♥ What you have discovered will help you respond to your (and others') feelings most intelligently. People can't remain angry or stressed when laughter is present; negativity dissolves. Allow yourself to choose the best in every circumstance. You deserve it.

EXERCISE #3 – Best Solutions to Everyday Challenges

In life there will always be obstacles. Your ultimate success in dealing with them depends on how you perceive them.

If you see those obstacles as annoyances you shouldn't have to endure, you create stress that will make the problem worse. Remember that emotional upheaval shuts down your frontal lobe. This exercise will help you manage challenges in the most productive way.

Think of a problem in your workplace. Answer the questions:

1. DEFINE THE PROBLEM: What adversity am I dealing with? What success am I not achieving?

2. Is this within my control? If not, how can I bring about the most optimal outcome?

3. What are my best options for solving the problem?

4. Am I willing to do all things necessary to create a favorable solution?

5. What is the first step?

♥ How can you apply what you discovered? Make a decision to do that now. You'll be delighted you did.

Get subconscious support: Say: *I now choose to believe consciously and subconsciously that:*

- *It is okay to do what is in my best interest*
- *I am grateful for my career*
- *I can handle whatever comes my way*

Now you have the best possible strategy for overcoming obstacles. How do you imagine yourself handling them from now on?

EXERCISE #4 - Optimizing Your Health

Your wellness affects your ability to manage a classroom. It affects your energy and your attendance. If you aren't totally healthy, you can't function at your peak.

This exercise will empower you to begin to care for yourself in the wisest way.

As you answer these questions consider your lifestyle in regard to diet, exercise, rest, and attitude.

1. What does peak health mean for me?

_____

_____

_____

2. Why is physical wellness in my best interest?

_____

_____

_____

3. What stops me from achieving it?

_____

_____

_____

4. What will help me attain it?

_____

_____

_____

5. Knowing that stress is caused not by situations but by our reactions to them, how can I train myself to react positively to challenging circumstances?

_____

_____

_____

6. How do I rid myself of the health-defeating tendency to impart negative meaning to events and circumstances?

_____

_____

_____

♥ These powerful affirmations will help you:
- *I choose to enjoy the best health possible at all times*
- *I choose to accept my body completely and make the most of it*
- *I love my entire system*

- *Am I making the wisest decisions about my health?*

Decide now to use them whenever you think of it. The more you love and care for yourself, the easier and faster you create optimal well-being.

PART TWO

THE ROLE OF EMOTION IN LEARNING

"THE BRAIN IS ORGANIZED TO PROCESS
EMOTION ALONG WITH LOGIC."
—*Restak*

You have a lot to teach and your students have a lot to learn. Success all around depends on two things: how your students feel about learning and how they feel about a particular subject. *Without positive feelings about learning and about the subject matter, students do not do well.* To change negative to positive, we need to understand how the mind works.

The mind files things by subject. When you want to achieve or obtain, negative feelings and beliefs come up. Example: a woman falls in love and is considering a relationship. Past experiences come to mind: the heartbreak her friend went through, her cousin's unfortunate marriage to a member of Escaped Ax Murderers Anonymous, and the continuing tragedy of national role model Kim Kardashian. The woman fears her new True Love has been prominently featured on the Jerry Springer show and is the defendant in a class-action suit brought by several thousand women who thought he was actually allowed by law to get married.

Many of your students feel the same way about school. Perhaps they failed tests. Or they made mistakes and got yelled at. Maybe a well-meaning teacher asked questions like *"What's wrong with you? Why are you always causing problems?"* Children painfully absorb negative messages, bury them in the psyche, and develop limiting beliefs: *"Something is wrong with me, learning is too hard, I can't..."*

Now they talk out of turn, throw knives at each other, threaten to report each other's parents to the IRS, refuse to do their work, lack motivation and bang their heads on their desks because it feels so good when they stop.

You're dealing with emotional brains. Your students operate from the amygdala. *It's all about how they feel* and the most important thing to them is feeling good.

The key is to create a positive learning atmosphere. Without it you "force" your students to misbehave. This is caused by mirror neurons. A mirror neuron fires when you act *and* when you observe that action performed by another. The neuron mirrors the behavior of the other as though the observer were acting.

Has a movie ever brought tears to your eyes? Mirror neurons make it possible for us to feel what others feel. Your students will mirror back to you your anger, your encouragement, your attitude toward them.

Example: at the door you see Maynard Gumbleton sauntering your direction. You remember Maynard. He's the one who said mean things to your classroom snake, told your husband why you and Mr. Johnson were really staying after school, and egged your house just because you gave him a well-deserved F on a history test. Your bowels suddenly feel kind of loose. You are hoping he knows nothing about that little episode in the basement last week involving you and Handyman Jack. He sees your face and glares as he brushes past you into the room, leaving a substance of unknown origin on your sleeve, although considering the trouble he has caused you, he should be grinning like an idiot.

You smile at Maynard. A nice big smile. He thinks the tears in your eyes are of joy at his return from a mandatory sixty-three day vacation courtesy of the local youth authority.

Choose to love Maynard. People who are hardest to love need love the most.

A negative frame of mind interferes with your ability to teach, forcing your students to go off task. You are their mirror. They look up and reflect your vibes. Their unhappy reaction to negativity: acting out in an attempt to find emotional relief. They are turned off to anything you have to say; you have lost them.

"Emotion decides what holds your attention." (Pert) Your students will react positively through what makes them feel good. How can you get them to feel good about learning? Move forward and discover the power you have to make learning a happy, productive, win-win experience in your classroom.

CHAPTER SIX

Change Negative Feelings about Learning

"GETTING OTHERS TO CHANGE IS EASIEST
WHEN WE ADOPT A NEW POWERFUL VIEW OF
OURSELVES AS INFLUENCERS."
—*Patterson, et al.*

You cannot help your students until they like learning. They experience events connected to learning in your classroom every day. Here's your opportunity.

Change what learning means for them. Ask, "*What is the real purpose of school?*" You'll gain tremendous insight from their answers. With that insight, you will be able to make learning a top priority. This occurs when learning becomes the gateway to their dreams.

Old perception claims good behavior facilitates learning. Not true. New perception is that *attitude* facilitates learning. This includes positive attitudes like curiosity, empowerment, hope, and actual enjoyment of the learning process.

In this chapter, you will discover:

+ How to create a positive attitude about learning
+ The secret to making your teaching irresistible
+ Easy ways to promote development of positive feeling
+ One of the most crippling beliefs about learning
+ How to magically inspire kids who say "I don't care!"

How ready are you to explore this powerful information now?

Positive Attitude

Imagine students walking into your classroom with a sign across their foreheads that asks *"What's in it for me?"* We all perform in response to this question. We work for pay and we help others because it makes us feel good. Students need the same motivation (reward, personal satisfaction) to study and learn.

On the first day of school, a good teacher sets a positive foundation by motivating the class. She asks, *why is this subject important?* and allows the students to express their understanding of the question.

Testing, Testing

This is NOT the time to talk about tests, which are a blitheringly ineffective motivator. Students don't like tests. (Duh.) But if students fall in love with a subject, testing becomes an opportunity to show off instead of an experiment in terror.

Example: explain to students that mastery of language will make them superb communicators. Teaching example: you want to be hired for a lucrative position or buy a new car. You need to know how to exercise language skills that will put what you want in your hands. Mastering language—spoken or written—gives you an edge.

The words that fall from your lips become irresistible when you make a distinction between *teaching students* and teaching a subject. Teachers of *students* know that the students are not there for the curriculum; the curriculum is there for the students. If your students are swinging from the chandeliers while you earnestly discourse on the importance of world history, you have fallen into the trap of teaching the curriculum.

Example: one teacher I know believes strongly in teaching the whole child: her students are taught manners, decorum, respect for one another, and assertiveness (say how you feel, ask for what you want). Her Christian values imbue her students with sensitivity, kindness, and love for oneself and others.

My Own Philosophy

I strongly believe the past does not determine the future, and the quality of the future is determined by the amount and quality of education we are willing to take into our own hands.

Here's a personal story. Some time ago I had a credit card debt over four years old. The collection agency took me to court. As I stood, ignorant of my rights, the judge read the charge. He stopped, peered over his glasses and waited for me to speak. The pleading look on his face made me suspect he wanted me to win this thing. I was fearful and tongue-tied. He shook his head sadly, pounded his gavel, and ruled against me.

Years later I learned there are laws to assist you in dealing with financial difficulties. If I had said, "The statute of limitation on this debt is expired," the judge would have dismissed the case and the debt. My legal ignorance cost me a great deal in embarrassment, time, and money.

Research shows that "integrating whole ideas—combining the heart and head is necessary for optimum learning." (Childre, et. al.) Share personal stories like the one above with your students. Give them a desire to master what you're teaching because it's important for their success—not just in school, but in life.

Positive Learning Exercise

On the first day of school, take your students through the following. Ask: *Why is it important to do well in school?* Or: *If you wanted to do well in school, why would you want to do well?* List their answers on the board

This is important: you've tapped into their powers of reasoning. And reasons are emotional. "One measure of student engagement is emotional and cognitive involvement with the course material." (Wang) Seeing their ideas listed, students become aware of reasons they hadn't thought of. Make a poster of the listed answers to refer to throughout the year. Powerful.

NOTE: If you didn't do this on day one, it's never too late. Try the beginning of the semester or quarter, month, or week. The point is to do it.

Teaching Irresistibly

When you attach your subject to your students' futures, you capture them. Example: A high school math teacher struggled with a lesson. Paper wads (and not a few condoms) flew across the room. They ignored the teacher and yelled at each other. Some had their heads on the desks, asleep. The teacher tried taking some of the more violent offenders outside for a private conference, the result of which the teacher now has a permanent limp. He told me he was seriously considering a new career as a carnival ride operator.

Three weeks later I sauntered quietly into the room. Students sat at rapt attention, eyes on the screen, pencils copying furiously. Some students called out, "Hey, Mr. T, what about the 'x,' how did you get that?" A room full of kids *wanted* information, almost begged for it. I shed tears of joy watching these bored, discouraged, unengaged kids actually excited about learning. Hanging on to the teacher's every word. A teacher's dream.

Many students feel powerless about their futures. They are trained to place their education in the hands of their teachers. Who decides what they learn? Who decides what grade they get? If they question the teacher, what happens? They get in trouble.

If you still have students who don't want to learn, you have not connected school to their future happiness. Ask your students: *what do you want to achieve in your life?* Show them how education will help them get it. Instruct them to keep their eyes on the goal.

Connecting education to their future well-being empowers your students and gives them an incentive to soak up all the knowledge they can hold.

Example: one teacher asks her teenage students, *Why do we have to learn math and algebra?* The kids usually don't have an answer. She explains to them, "When you grow up and are hugely successful, you have to know where your money is. You have to know your accountant isn't planning to run off to South America with it, your kids aren't lifting it from your wallet, your wife isn't spending it on the pool boy, and your secretary isn't embezzling from the office to buy that mink coat you promised her in a weak moment during the office Christmas party. You have to know how much interest you're paying on the mortgage of your oversized McMansion, your overpriced car, and the status labels your wife insists on wearing to impress her image-obsessed friends."

The emotional association of learning with money, happiness, and the prospect of a good future will go a long way to motivating your students. The idea is learn now, get paid later.

Coaching Students into Better Feelings

Sometimes students come to school angry or sad because of negative experience at home. This blocks their ability to focus. It's important to *always* put students in a positive state of mind before the school day begins.

If your students are not in a mood conducive to learning, you've lost them. They will distract themselves by throwing spit wads, talking out of turn, cracking jokes, or setting your desk on fire. The teacher's reaction: You are disturbing the class. The correct reaction: There are negative feelings here. (Gee, ya think?)

At a seminar I asked teachers: "When you're feeling down, what do you do to make yourself feel better?" I got several responses: run, go to the gym, listen to music, sleep, eat.

We all have ways of self-medicating. Some are healthful, others not so. And your students are doing what they know how to relieve their emotional unease.

A fifth grader known for his explosive temper frantically paced the school yard. The principal called him over. He strode to us with furrowed brow and tight fists.

I asked, "How are you feeling right now?" He responded through clenched teeth that he was mad because a girl was calling him names. I calmly said, "I know what you mean," paused briefly and said, "Go to a better feeling." He took a deep breath and his shoulders relaxed. The principal looked at me in astonishment.

"What do you want?" I asked the boy.

"I want her to leave me alone."

"What have you already tried?"

"I told her to stop and I told the teacher but she just won't stop."

"What's a better way to get what you want?" I asked.

He thought about it. "I can set up a meeting with the teacher."

We discussed positive ways of handling negative situations and he left feeling empowered and happy.

Later the principal explained that this boy had been through unhappy experiences (at home and at school) which had brought on the angry outbursts no one had been able to deal with. She vowed to use this powerful strategy in the future.

Help your students shift into a positive state with ease. Here's how: *Speak directly to the subconscious.*

You're feeling angry.
Stop feeling that way and go to a better feeling now.

Emotion sends words to the subconscious and influences conscious behavior. Amazing.

Influencing Children

Teachers influence without saying anything. Their attitudes preach a sermon. Konstantopoulos suggests that the effects of teachers on students remain strong predictors of achievement. Sadly, some teachers do not expect students to succeed. A powerful study by J. Rosenthal has demonstrated that you create what you expect.

He split a group of students who tested average into two classes. He told one teacher that her students weren't very bright and probably wouldn't go far. The other group he described as intelligent late bloomers who would do extremely well.

At the end of the year, the students labeled intelligent scored much higher than before. The other students performed below their previous average level. Your teachers' subconscious expectations control you.

You get what you expect because you behave in a way that invites the same expectation from others. Example: you think your cousin Harold is a loser. In 1987 he got fired from his job as a Christmas tree salesman, and two years later his wife left him for a guy selling vacuums door-to-door. He fell off a curb while hailing a taxi and ruptured his spleen in four places and got food poisoning from drinking bottled water, which left him with urophobia (an unnatural fear of other people's kidneys).

Now Harold wants to borrow money from you to pay for a course in bicycle repair. You hand him $50, look him in the eye, and say, "Harold, you're a loser so I know I'm never gonna see this money again."

That was ten years ago and you're still waiting for your $50.

This is the power of the Law of Expectation.

Expectation causes two things: you experience the feelings that accompany the event and you behave *as if* it has already happened. It occurs. This is the power of your subconscious belief system.

 Here's an important question: What do you believe about your students and their ability to learn? Unless you have high expectations you will get low results. Your kids are looking into you, taking their cues from you. Choose to believe they can learn, behave well, and succeed.

What do your students believe about themselves and their abilities? If they perceive themselves as incapable, intellectually inferior, socially inept, or emotionally unable to cope, you have the power to help change these false perceptions.

Empowering Questions

Ask your students: *Why do students think they can't learn?* Make this powerful suggestion: *That's only a belief—if you believe you can't you can't and if you believe you can you can. And from now on you'll believe you can. And I am going to teach you some tricks that will help you learn fast.*

The following questions will get the same results. If a student says, "It's too hard," ask, *"What would happen if you believed the opposite?"* You'll be amazed at how well this question works. Here are some other examples:

1. *What is it like when you're at your best in school?*

2. *What if you believed you could learn any subject faster and easier? How would your school life be different?*

3. *How do you know when you're feeling confident? What is it like when you're feeling extremely confident?*

4. *Imagine what it is like to be totally successful in school. What are you doing? What are you telling yourself? How does it feel?*

5. *How do you know when you feel positive, strong, and happy?*

Remember, you don't have to wait for a response—the mind (and behavior) will reply.

Teach Students to Believe in Constant Improvement

One of the most crippling beliefs about learning is "I should know this already." The most powerful fear is the fear of making mistakes or being wrong. This fear stops us from learning.

Students beat themselves up: *I shouldn't have to study so much.* They ask negative questions like: *What's wrong with me? Why can't I get this right? Am I dumb or what?* When negative answers come, the brain reverts to a reptilian level. (Write your own punchline here.)

Teach students what success is: neverending improvement. When they allow themselves room to grow, they learn fast and easy and feel good about themselves.

Improving Student Self Talk

"Students limit their academic performance by engaging in negative self-talk about their abilities." (Linnenbrink & Pintrich) How does this happen?

Your subconscious makes true what it hears three or four times. If a student says "learning is hard," his mind will work tirelessly to prove it. He'll find himself forgetting things, struggling through assignments, feeling defeated.

Teach students to use self-talk to incur success in school and in life. Here are some ways to help them:

1. Have them make a list of their best qualities and review and add to it each week.

2. Put up Optimistic Boomerang Words around the room (achieve, choice, humor, improve, smart, success, results, release, happy, safe, free). Weave them into your daily instruction and encourage students to use them.

3. Use the Cancel Factor. If they slip and call themselves (or anyone else) names or make negative comments, teach them to say *I cancel that*. Stating it within fourteen seconds keeps negativity from setting up shop in the subconscious and demeaning their behavior.

Magically Inspire "I don't care" Kids

A child's biggest fear is of losing his teacher's approval. Example: a child gets out of his seat without permission. The teacher screams at him. He feels diminished. After experiencing this a few times he shields himself. "I don't care" means "I'm protecting myself from pain."

Some children have never had a teacher who believed in them and helped them feel good about themselves. Now we're dealing with the painful results. The good news is, it's not too late to influence these children for good. Did you know that it takes nineteen positive statements to counteract one negative one?

Use these empowering messages:

- *I understand you don't care, but I believe in you. And you can now choose to believe in yourself too*

- *What if you did care because you wanted to be successful not only in school but in life—what would be different?*

- *What if you knew that you are powerful enough to care and to learn fast and easy? What would you do next?*

This strategy works only when you believe it will. And you can now choose to believe it will work with ease and speed because you're an outstanding professional who wants the highest good for your students. Congratulations!

HOW TO EASILY APPLY IT

1. Help your students create a positive attitude toward their power to learn.

2. Connect your subject to their future happiness; this makes your teaching irresistible.

3. If a child comes to school in a state of emotional negativity, coach him into a better feeling.

4. Use questions to change students' limiting beliefs to empowering ones.

5. Teach students to believe in constant improvement; to realize they *have* to make mistakes in order to learn, so they can let themselves off the hook.

6. Decide now to inspire kids who say "I don't care."

CHAPTER SEVEN

Apply Universal Life Motivators to the Classroom

"THE DREAM BEGINS, MOST OF THE TIME, WITH A TEACHER WHO BELIEVES IN YOU, WHO TUGS AND PUSHES AND LEADS YOU ON TO THE NEXT PLATEAU, SOMETIMES POKING YOU WITH A SHARP STICK CALLED TRUTH."
—Dan Rather

To get your students to beg for more of what you have to teach, you must understand the real job of a teacher. *It is to create an environment that makes it easy for students to learn and be motivated.*

Why is it the teacher's job? If students were intrinsically motivated, they wouldn't need teachers. Intrinsic motivation drives you to what excites you. Motivation, especially for the offspring of parents trying to survive, *has to come from the teacher.*

Motivation creates effort. You do what you do because you want to. You eat that nine-hundred calorie pizza with no nutritional content whatsoever because you want to. You go home and polish off two six-packs of Miller Lite to recover from your day at school because you want to. Your students will learn when they want to. And you can get them to want to. Your mindset must be: *If a student does not learn, the teacher has not taught.*

This may not seem logical considering the annoying behavior teachers have to put up with in the classroom, but the teacher must believe it's true and behave as if it is true to be optimally effective.

In this chapter, you will discover:

- The Four Universal Life Motivators
- Trigger words that drive people to action
- Easy ways to apply Trigger Statements
- The power of identity

Universal Motivators

Some students are motivated in the home. Caribbean students come to America to study, and some Latino parents believe education is the way up. Many kids attend school only because the law demands it. A single working mother's first priority is survival and she is often unable to model the importance of education.

There are students from the hood who have been told to forget it, the white man won't let them succeed. They see pimps rolling in Caddies through the neighborhood. They observe the fame and fortune of sports figures and mistakenly believe crime and fame are their only way up.

It is *essential* that students from less than ideal backgrounds understand and value what education will do for their lives. They need the strongest motivation possible.

Here are the motivators and they apply in life as well as in school.

1. Recognition – respect and a positive place among our

peers.

2. Money - we hang on to and increase our financial resources.

3. Self-preservation – doing what is necessary to *survive* and *thrive.*

4. Romance – it's more than love; it's a desire for and enjoyment of new ventures, new ideas, new directions.

Everyone has a primary motivator. Use all four with your students. Show them how they will gain or lose by learning or not learning. Students may not understand, so demonstrate and model.

A high school math teacher did this beautifully. Before teaching the steps to solving a quadratic equation, he gave the students a tax form. He told them the better they followed the steps, the easier it would be to keep the IRS from taking their money (loss of income; self-preservation). He inspired them by telling them that when they follow steps well they will be paid good sums of money to do other people's taxes (money, recognition).

Those students sat on the edge of their seats learning the steps of the quadratic formula. When you motivate you get surprising results.

What motivated you to become a teacher?

Trigger Words

We all have motivational filters that drive and inspire us to do what we do. (Bandler, et. al)

One filter is direction. Some of us are motivated *toward* pleasure; we want to achieve. Others are motivated *away from* problems or pain; they want to avoid trouble. Knowing what direction motivates your students greatly increases your chances that they will seek to achieve.

Words give insight into direction. People moving toward pleasure use words like *I want some of that, can you get it for me wholesale, that hot tub with those expensive looking, semi-dressed women looks good.* People running from pain use words like *scared spitless, get the heck outta here, do you think anybody saw me?*

Here is a list of trigger words for each direction. Season your instruction with words from both because you have students with both filters.

Toward	Away From
Have	Avoid
Get	Deadlines
Achieve	Eliminate
Attain	Get rid of
Pleasure	Pain
Goal	Prevent
Be able to	There will be no problems
Benefits	Not have to deal with
Advantages	Won't have to

In Your Experience – *Applying Trigger Statements*

Suppose you want to use a direction filter to motivate your students. Practice now by reading each statement. Label it either "T" for Toward, "AW," for Away From, or "B" for Both.

1. _____Doing your work now means more free time later.

2. _____Doing well in school makes it easier to attain goals in life.

3. _____Doing your schoolwork can help you get your parents off your back.

4. _____The more you learn in books, the less you get cheated in life.

5. _____A good education promotes future happiness.

6. _____When you pay attention to me, you gain privileges and avoid a trip to the principal's offices escorted by two armed

guards.

7. _____The smarter your behavior, the more respect you get from your peers.

8. _____ Do the right thing now and feel good about yourself and prevent problems.

9. _____Are things bad enough now to make a change or do you want to wait until they are even worse?

(Answers: 1. T, 2. T, 3. AW, 4. AW, 5. T, 6. B, 7. T, 8. B, 9. AW)

The Power of Identity

People do what they do because of who they think they are. "When kids play video games, winning becomes more than just the challenge of reaching the next level. It becomes a measure of who they are." (Patterson et. al.) What does this mean for you?

When learning aligns with a student's desired self-image, the results are compelling. In one classroom a large poster proclaims: SMART PEOPLE READ A LOT! Do your students want to be smart, helpful, successful, rich, cool? Find out. Then attach learning goals to those desires.

Teach Life

Two of the most important values in America are a sense of belonging and a sense of connection. Satisfaction of these psychological needs insures satisfaction of primary needs (food, shelter, water, rest).

Teach students that future jobs will consist primarily of relationships. Good communication skills foster and promote approval, acceptance, control, and security, forging mutually beneficial relationships and guarantee that primary needs are met.

Teach by example and precept. Example: when a teacher says "I want you to do what I say," he is teaching cooperation, which is the basis of a good life. The teacher needs to make that point. Divorces, lawsuits, feuds, and double homicides occur because people are unable and/or unwilling to cooperate. If you live in a place where you frequently interact with law enforcement, it's important that you cooperate (even if you don't want to) so you don't end up doing one to five for obstructing justice.

If you catch students participating in unwanted behavior, teach life.

Success Story

A teenager was in trouble for turning out the lights, not doing his work, goofing around. The principal asked me to speak with him.

I asked, "What do you want to achieve in life?"

He responded, "I want to be a millionaire. I want to take care of my kids and family."

"What else do you want?"

"I want to buy a house."

"I believe you were acting up to attract, create, and cement friendships, and that's important to you. But you have to do it in a certain context. You don't make jokes and laugh at funerals, you don't talk in class when the teacher is talking."

He nodded and smiled.

I continued, "If you saw yourself as a young millionaire, how would you behave in class?"

"I'd be quiet, do my work and mind the teacher."

"A successful life means getting what you want. You come to school so you can learn what you need to know for your future happiness.

"A good life is based on cooperation. When the teacher asks you to do something, she is teaching you how to cooperate. People hit dead ends in life because they never learned to cooperate. In the community, you need to cooperate with authority so you can be Student of the Month at Liverwood High instead of Employee of the Month at Guido's Famous Greaseburgers or Inmate of the Month at County Jail.

"Authority is power," I explained, "and if you rebel, you lose the game. They can send you home, suspend you, or expel you, and there goes the education a young millionaire needs.

"So what are you willing to do?"

He strode into the principal's office and announced, "I want to go back to the classroom and prove I can cooperate with authority. I have a new mindset." (Yes, those were his exact words.)

He became a millionaire in his mind and acted accordingly. Make students aware that they can become who they want to be and that school is the vehicle that will take them where they want to go. Empowering.

HOW TO EASILY APPLY IT

1. Create an environment that makes it easy for students to learn.

2. Teach LIFE: motivationally. You are teaching students, not a subject. Use the Four Universal Life Motivators: show, tell, and demonstrate how students will gain or lose as a result of learning (or not) what you're teaching.

3. Some students are motivated toward pleasure and others away from pain. Sprinkle your instruction with trigger words from both directions.

4. Never allow students to label themselves with limiting language (I'm dumb, I'm a failure, I'm not good enough).

   Teach them to identify with their successful future selves (master technician, millionaire, entrepreneur, U.S. President, clothing designer).

   Challenge students to choose who they will become. Have them write three reasons it's important to be that new person. When you get their "whys," attach them to the learning goals you have for them. Happily watch what happens next.

CHAPTER EIGHT

Closing the Gap:
Easy Ways to Increase Achievement Among Blacks and Latinos

"A MULTISENSORY APPROACH USUALLY LEADS TO
GREATER SUCCESS IN LEARNING
—Gurian

While a seventh-grade English teacher presented a lesson, a black student got up and walked the entire perimeter of the classroom. He went down one side of the room, across the back, up the other side, crossed right in front of the still-talking teacher, and took his seat.

Later she explained that this boy was easily distracted. She struggled to get him to stay focused, and he was sent from the classroom several times a week.

I explained that certain learners get in trouble because of their representational system. Behaviors like calling out, leaving a seat without permission, and interrupting the teacher are often interpreted as rude, distractive, or defiant. *Teachers who view these behaviors as an expression of a student's representational system are better able to remain calm and find a solution to the problem.*

In this chapter, you will discover:

- How representational systems affect learning
- Ways to avoid cross-communication (disharmony)
- Easy teaching strategies that appeal to all systems

How Representational Systems Affect Learning

In the '70s, Bandler and Grinder studied how people perceive and interact with the world. One concept is Representational Systems.

Representational systems employ our five senses to process information and experience and interpret the world. Each of us prefers some senses over others.

Knowing your students' thinking and learning strategies can give you insight into helping them succeed. To understand how representational systems affect learning, we need to discuss something you might find surprising about the traditional education system. Read on.

The Traditional Educational System

American education is geared to audio-visual learners. Teachers talk (auditory) and use visual strategies like writing on the board. Audio-visual presupposes that *all* students will thereby process information. This causes two problems:

(1) Students have difficulty understanding what the teacher says. (2) Students become restless, which creates discipline problems. How does this happen?

The student can't understand because the teacher is communicating in a way the student doesn't process. The student, confused and bored, will talk, pinch someone, start cracking jokes. The teacher misinterprets his behavior as defiance and punishes him. She says things like "You are distracting the class."

The student is merely distracting *himself* from the negativity brought on by lack of comprehension. This creates a disruptive atmosphere.

Twenty plus years of experience has taught me that most black and Latino Americans are kinesthetic—they learn intuitively, which is the number one cause of the Achievement Gap. Study the following chart and you'll understand why.

VAK Systems Behavioral Chart

	Kinesthetic	Auditory	Visual
Learn best by:	doing, hands-on experiences	hearing, discussions	seeing, looking at demonstrations
If inactive:	moves, touches objects at random	talks, drums on desk	stares into space; draws or doodles
Recalls best:	what was done	what is heard	what is seen
Enjoys/needs:	action, movement, wiggling, space	music, debates, conversation	movies, reading, staring, doodling
Gets pulled off task or defocused by:	unfinished tasks, movement, having to sit still for long periods	sounds, noise	messiness, lack of visual order
When feeling stressed or pressured:	moves	talks	freezes
Approaches problems or tasks:	avoids planning, jumps right in, thinks about it later	needs to talk it out	likes to plan and organize, check off lists

Notice that when kinesthetics do nothing too long, they lose focus. Note what distracts them—movement in the room *and* sitting for long periods.

Kinesthetics, upon receiving directions, will move: rummage in backpacks, get up to sharpen a pencil, sit down, put paper in the trash, sit down. They are processing instruction.

Did you know that many of these learners get mislabeled as ADD?

Connecting Learning Behaviors to VAK Systems

Read the examples below and check the spaces under the VAK Style (visual, auditory, kinesthetic) it most closely matches. Use figure A for hints. (There are four checks for each style. Answers follow.)

Behavior	Representational System		
	V	A	K
1. Finds touch important	____	____	____
2. Finds appearance important	____	____	____
3. Hums or talks to self	____	____	____
4. Learns by seeing	____	____	____
5. Likes reading aloud	____	____	____
6. Gestures when speaking	____	____	____
7. Remembers what was said	____	____	____
8. Reacts restlessly to instruction	____	____	____
9. Touches words when reading	____	____	____
10. Is more quiet than others	____	____	____
11. Is usually organized	____	____	____
12. Is distracted by noise	____	____	____

(Exercise 1—Answers: 1.K 2.V 3.A 4.V 5.A 6.K 7.A 8.K 9.K 10.V 11.V 12.A)

Which of these behaviors describe you? Teachers teach in accordance with their perceptions. As a good teacher you want to be able to handle all three. The following information will help.

In Your Experience

Auditory Learner

- Learns by hearing and discussion
- Drums on table, debates (argues) well
- Likes to talk, may get in trouble for talking too much

Who does this remind you of and why?

_____

_____

Kinesthetic Learner

- Moves a lot, action oriented
- The entertainer
- May get in trouble for getting out of seat

Who does this remind you of and why?

_____

_____

Visual Learner

- Learns by seeing
- More quiet and organized
- Can sit still for long periods of time

Who does this remind you of and why?

_____

_____

Understand that certain behavior signals a mismatch between a student's perception and your teaching style.

We've gotten the idea that a quiet class is a productive one. A quiet class is also indicative of a dead one. To keep students engaged, change the way you present information. If you've been imparting it verbally, write something on the board and have them copy it. Or play a game. Move or change your position. Have them move or change their positions.

An eighth grade math teacher was explaining parabolas. Students yawned, sighed, and stared into space. Several chatted in the back row. Suddenly the teacher threw her arms up in the air and made a strange sound. The students snapped to attention. They looked up to see her arms overhead in the shape of a big U. Excitement in her voice, she exclaimed, "PA-RA-BO-LA!" She drew the word out almost as if singing it.

Kids started laughing. She had them. Moments later they were doing it too. Standing, arms outstretched to the sky. "PA-RA-BO-LA!" They echoed her enthusiasm.

The teacher led them in another chorus. "PA-RA-BO-LA! One girl said, "I feel like I'm in church!" The room erupted in laughter. They all remembered it on the test. "A joyful classroom atmosphere makes students more apt to learn how to successfully solve problems in potentially stressful situations." (Sylvester)

Instruct in ways that include all sensory systems and you reach your students. This applies everywhere, not just in the classroom. It applies in your home, in the workplace, and in relationships. It shapes your thinking, behavior, even language.

Sensory Specific Language

People who get along well speak the same language. We characterize our experiences through our senses. If you and your students use different systems to communicate, you'll have conflict. Why is that?

We understand words in different ways. We communicate via perception that is natural to us. This becomes our dominant (conscious) system.

We speak and understand through our conscious system. The other two are subconscious. We use sensory specific words that match our dominant system.

Example: visual people say things like:

I *see* what you mean.
Will you *show* me how?
It's *clear* to me now.

If you are auditory you say things like:
I *hear* what you're *saying*.
That *sounds* good.
Tell me what you mean.

Kinesthetics "feel" what's happening in their world. They are likely to say:
That *feels* right.
Let's stay in *touch*.
That story made an *impact* on me.

(The language of taste and smell fit in this category too.
I have expensive *tastes*.
Ah! The sweet *smell* of success.)

Cross Communication Equals Disharmony

If a teacher uses one system and the student responds in another, you have misunderstanding and conflict. Here's a conversation between Mr. Smith and Mary:

Visual Mr. Smith: Do you see what I mean?
Auditory Mary: That doesn't sound right to me.

Here's another example.

> Kinesthetic Mike: I just can't seem to grasp this idea.
> Auditory Mrs. Jones: Were you listening when I explained?

People who don't understand one another usually don't get along. *What is often perceived as racism or ethnic intolerance is actually misunderstanding caused by differing perception.*

When dealing with communication filters, people often misread signals and make judgments and inferences based on imagination, which I have found to be about seventy-eight percent incorrect. Avoid this unnecessary trouble by recognizing sensory specific words and phrases. Here are some common ones.

Common VAK Words and Phrases

Visual	Auditory	Kinesthetic
See, focus, picture, look, bright, blank, vision, perspective, insight, illuminate, clearly, color	Discuss, ask, debate, talk, vocalize, harmony, shout, yell, argue, outspoken, question	Cool, touch, feel, movement, hot, pushy, firm, solid, bounce, flow, grasp, moved, exciting
We're seeing eye-to-eye	*That is music to my ears*	*Keep in touch*
I look forward to seeing you	*Sounds good*	*That hit home*
Tunnel vision	*Word for word*	*I get the impression*
Sight for sore eyes	*I heard it straight from her mouth*	*Hold on to*
Saw a glimpse into the future	*Listen up*	*It feels right*
		Made an impact

"SINCE WE LIVE IN A COMPOSITE WHOLE-
BRAIN WORLD, AND THE REALITY OF ANY
MULTIFUNCTIONAL GROUP IS THE DIVERSITY
OF ITS THINKING AND, THEREFORE, ITS
PERCEPTIONS AND LANGUAGE, IT IS ESSENTIAL
FROM A COMMUNICATIONS STANDPOINT
TO INCREASE OUR TOLERANCE OF AND
UNDERSTANDING OF WHAT PEOPLE ARE SAYING
WHO ARE DIFFERENT FROM US"
—Herrmann,[not Munster]

Teaching Strategies that Appeal to ALL VAKs

1. Alternate frequently between talking and having students talk to each other.

2. Use gestures and body coding as you teach. Have students gesture and speak with you.

3. Have students dictate concepts to a partner. The partner writes it down and vice versa.

4. Tell a short story to demonstrate your point.

5. Connect concepts to popular music and movies.

6. Use diagrams, graphs, and maps. Explain them. Have students repeat what you say.

7. When reading aloud, vary it. You read a little. Small groups read (boys, girls, people wearing jeans, people who like pizza), whole class stands and reads, etc.

How will you use this information to help your students learn better?

_____

_____

What two strategies would you enjoy using most this week?

_____

_____

Your SUBCONSCIOUS Expectations

Students especially respond to subconscious expectations. Mrs. Sykentyred struggled with a group of black students in the back every day. They yelled across the room, talked back, cursed. They refused to do any work. Some key questions uncovered limiting beliefs. She was shocked to discover that she believed black and Latino students are not sharp.

She changed her belief on the subject; her students began to engage her in polite conversation, behave in the classroom, and turn in markedly improved work.

In another school teachers complained that girls were underperforming. They refused to participate, they turned in inferior work. It was discovered that teachers expected more from boys than girls. They called on boys more; demanded more from them; sent them to the office twice as often as girls. They didn't realize they presented a double standard in the classroom.

Teachers need to examine their thinking and rid themselves of all limiting expectations.

HOW TO EASILY APPLY IT

Make your language compelling:

1. When you talk with someone, match his system.

2. When you teach, use predicates from all three.

3. Give directions one at a time. You can tell a visual, "After you do this, do that." To kinesthetics, such directions confuse and distract.

4. Connect what you teach to the senses. Have students draw it, describe the sounds associated with it, act it out, etc.

5. Make sure you get rid of any limiting expectations for *all* students—black, female, Latino, white, Eskimo, lily-white, albino...

   - Ask yourself: *What do I believe about these students and their ability to learn? What do I believe about their behavior? Do I believe they can/will cooperate?* If negative answers arise, release them.

   - Choose to believe the positive opposite. Example: you believe some students won't cooperate. Say: *I choose to believe these students will cooperate. And I release everything to the contrary.* When you have high expectations for all your students, you communicate your confidence in their ability to learn.

6. Tell real life stories of previous students and others who have successfully applied what they learned in the classroom.

CHAPTER NINE

Strategies for Instant Learning

"WE CANNOT SOLVE OUR PROBLEMS WITH THE
SAME THINKING WE USED WHEN WE CREATED
THEM. YOU HAVE TO LEARN THE RULES OF THE
GAME. AND THEN YOU HAVE TO PLAY BETTER
THAN ANYONE ELSE."

—Einstein

The brain is designed to learn. Unfortunately, some students' brains learn to feel trapped in school, to dread learning, to feel helpless, to believe that school is painful. What if you could get your students to learn so fast they would be amazed?

Since learning occurs in the subconscious, you have to be able to get there. If you want students to learn quickly and easily, use educational psychology. Learning by rote is the only psychology taught and unfortunately the least effective.

There are more effective ways to learn. You can learn in an instant through fear, shock, confusion, and pleasure. Example: how are phobias developed? One little exposure to a man-eating python and you develop a fear of snakes. If you enjoy a first kiss, how long does it take to learn how? Repetition, mistakenly considered a superior learning tool, is less than effective because it is not pleasurable to students.

Why pleasure instead of fear? Retention of learning requires revival of the accompanying emotion. An angry learner will feel anger when he remembers what he learned. The subconscious, primarily concerned with survival and well-being, hesitates to resurrect negative feeling associated with learning.

There is a saying that what we learn with pleasure we never forget. Negativity induces the subconscious to block what was learned.

We (especially parents and teachers) unconsciously create feelings. Parents put negatives into a child's mind after they hit him. "I don't know where I got you from, you're a disgrace." Hit, pain, fear: the child learns he is a disgrace and a deserving recipient of the abuse he receives.

Reprimanding a child to promote learning, in the home or in school, is tantamount to shooting yourself in the foot. Better approach: create a pleasurable learning environment.

In this chapter you will discover:

- How to create an effective learning environment and make you and your students happy (especially you)
- Easy ways to counteract boredom
- Five feel-good learning experiences that enhance comprehension and retention

A Consistent Learning Environment

You need to understand the Four Learning Stages:

1. Unconscious Incompetence—many of your students are here. They don't know that they don't know, so there is no motivation to learn.

2. Conscious Incompetence—motivation takes place when students realize there is something they need to know and don't.

3. Conscious Competence—learning always has to start here.

4. Unconscious Competence—They automatically do it well. You want them here. Students often want to be here without practicing. They want quick results.

Remember when you learned to drive? You discovered and practiced each detail—looking in rear and side view mirrors, using correct pressure on accelerator and brake, etc. You learned consciously and now you drive with unconscious competence.

How do you get your students to where learning starts?

- Decide what you want them to learn

- Give a pretest

- Make them conscious of their incompetence. Say: *You don't know this yet and it's important for you to know it.*

American schools focus on content. The *process* of learning is considered most important. When students know *how* to learn more than what to learn, greater achievement and equity take place.

This works even better when you leave no room for boredom, a state induced by:

1) Attending school (especially public school)
2) Not being allowed to annoy the teacher
3) Family members who have nothing to say and keep saying it
4) Listening to a teacher drone on about his past life as the imaginary friend of Bill Gates
5) Hanging out with kids who also have no friends and don't know what's going on with kids who do

A good teacher makes the classroom an interesting place. Interest depends upon how you answer the musical question *What's in it for me?*

Your students have two needs: a need for stimulation and a need for meaning. If these needs are not met, students become bored and cause problems. Remember, students operate from the emotional brain. You couldn't care less how your students feel, but they do and you have to deal with them all day.

The Need for Stimulation

Whether your students are introverts or extroverts depends on how they receive stimulation. Extroverts are all over the classroom, connecting, engaging with others, and causing all the trouble they can before dinnertime. Energized by what is going on, they think out loud, burp out loud, pass gas out loud, and annoy introverts out loud. Their energy is sapped by working independently, following directions, giving a rat's behind about their fellow students, or actually getting any work done.

In one middle school classroom, after students worked independently for twenty-five minutes the teacher told them to read silently for twenty minutes. Kids began to talk, she scolded them and it got worse. Other kids told inappropriate, off-color jokes and made obscene gestures at the principal, who was peeking in the window to see if the teacher might be available after class to discuss her Personal Performance Evaluation.

You can avoid problems like these by allowing extroverts time to work with others. Example: instead of going right into another independent activity (silent reading), the teacher above could have had the students work with a partner or in a small group to compare their answers while she emailed the principal to tell him she was quite satisfied with his Personal Performance.

(NOTE TO STAFF: The importance of stimulation in education cannot be overestimated.)

Balance is the key, so putting students in small groups all the time won't work either. Introverts are stimulated by what goes on in their minds. They become drained working with others (especially obnoxious extroverts) and need to restore their own energy. They are more reflective. Traditional education favors the introvert.

Students reflect, read, and write often. To help all students get needed stimulation, balance those activities with interactive lessons.

Providing for the Need for Meaning

Research supports meaningful learning. (Bransford, Brown, & Cocking) *What does it mean for me?* goes through students' minds continually. If your teaching doesn't answer that question, you lose their attention and they lose their motivation.

Avoid this issue. Before you teach, present a real life problem and ask them for the best solution. Then use content to make your point.

I was teaching my sixth graders Latin roots. I asked, "Do you know your friends don't always understand what you say because people don't give the same meaning to words? Street meanings are often different from book meanings."

That got their attention. I continued. "So what's the best way to make sure your friends understand you?" I noticed something interesting. Several slouchers in the back sat up in their seats, raised their eyebrows, and looked at me. I had been trying to get these students involved for weeks.

I continued to bring up the subject of talking, relationships with friends, etc. Pretty soon they were adding their own comments and stories of communication blunders. I had one hundred percent participation during the whole fifty-minute lesson. You can have this too when you make it fun. There are some excellent examples at the end of the chapter.

In Your Experience

1. What is the difference between teaching and talking?

    _____

    _____

    _____

2. What is the difference between listening and learning?

    _____

    _____

    _____

3. Which of these four quotes is similar to what you believe?

    > *I am in politics because of the struggle between good
    > and evil. I believe in the end good will triumph.*
    > *~Margaret Thatcher*

    > *Unless someone like you cares a whole lot, nothing's
    > going to get better; it's not. ~Dr. Seuss*

    > *When life gives you lemons, make lemonade.*
    > *~Unknown*

    > *You can't wake a person pretending to be asleep.*
    > *~Navajo Proverb*

*I am in politics because I'm a crook who wants to fool the public
all the time and retire with a bloated and largely undeserved
pension.*
> *~(Name your own government representative here)*

These quotes share some philosophies. Now it's your turn.

Describe your philosophy.

_____

_____

_____

HOW TO EASILY APPLY IT

1. Make students conscious of their incompetence (lack of knowledge or skill). Give a pretest and emphasize the importance of learning the material.

2. Persuade them that learning what you teach is enjoyable and in their best interest. Before you teach, make feel-good statements like:

    - *Ladies and Gentlemen, the only reason you've had trouble with_____ before is because you've never had me as a teacher.* (Smile evilly after each statement)

    - *You are about to discover how enjoyable learning really is.*

    - *Imagine what it is like to actually enjoy learning something new.*

    - *Pretend you really like learning something new and pay attention to what I'm about to say.*

3. Inject your philosophy into your teaching. It's important to have one; it makes the subject come alive. Show how the subject affects life today and in the future. This creates passion. When your passion shines through, your kids stay engaged longer and develop a love of learning.

4. Make learning a positive experience. Have students bring pictures of things they enjoy doing. Put them on your walls. Connect the concepts you teach to the pictures.

I shared this idea with an eighth grade history teacher. I suggested she put up a cartoon at the beginning of her lesson. She was skeptical but agreed to do it. She reported that she had more participation, more comments and answers demonstrating critical thinking than she'd ever witnessed. And when the bell rang to signal class was over, some kids even said, "Awww!"

Learning Experiences that Enhance Comprehension and Retention

1. Scavenger hunts or gallery walks—students leave their desks to walk around the room looking at posted information on walls, ceilings, etc., to find answers to worksheet questions. (Excellent for comprehensive review)

2. Share and learn—students write down one thing they learned from your lesson, then go around the room and exchange ideas, copying what their classmates have written (5-7 minutes). Reconvene and share with class.

3. Graffiti wall—post about ten big sheets, each with a question, around the room. Students write their names and answers on post-its and affix them to the wall sheets.

   Variations:

   - Post the answers. Students make up questions to go with answers and put them on each answer sheet.

   - Post topic sheets. Students circulate and write one thing they learned about the topic

   - Put open books on different desks. Open books to pages where answers are. Students go around finding and filling in answers to questions on their worksheets

4. Mix and match—each student works with a partner. One has a list of questions, the other a list of answers. They work together to match answers to questions. (Ten questions or less work best).

5. Four corners—put an activity in each corner of the room. When students finish an assignment they go to a corner and get an activity to complete.

These activities work even better when you structure the fun. The next chapter provides valuable information on how.

CHAPTER TEN

How to Have Structured Fun while Avoiding Chaos

IF ALL THE INFORMATION IN THIS ROOM ENTERED YOUR BRAIN AT ONCE, YOU'D GO CRAZY. "THE FUNCTION OF THE BRAIN AND NERVOUS SYSTEM IS TO PROTECT US FROM BEING OVERWHELMED AND CONFUSED BY THIS MASS OF LARGELY USELESS AND IRRELEVANT KNOWLEDGE, AND LEAVING ONLY THAT VERY SMALL AND SPECIAL SELECTION WHICH IS LIKELY TO BE PRACTICALLY USEFUL."
—Aldous Huxley

My work as a consultant has taken me into more than one thousand classrooms. And I have discovered that what stops teachers from having more fun in class is the fear of losing control. When control is lost, students waste time or put off getting started. They talk too loud. They don't complete tasks. They get up without permission or throw things.

What can you do? The surprising solution is to provide *structured fun*. This satisfies at least two cognitive filters: options vs. procedures. This comes from the concept of metaprograms conceived by Leslie Camron-Bandler and addresses the way behavior and language patterns reflect mental processes.

People with *option* filters see the whole picture and are concerned with the end result. All they need is a few examples and they take off. They are not necessarily more intelligent than other students, they just have a different filter.

Students who have a *procedure* filter like sequence. They are concerned with the how and need steps. If you tell them what to do without showing them, they get lost. Example: if I wanted you to call me, I'd say pick up the phone, find my number, and dial it. It may seem elementary, but that's how the mind processes information.

In this chapter you will discover:

- How brain filters affect learning behaviors
- Chunking down for success
- Using step charts successfully
- What to do when they go off task

Filters Affect Behaviors

Teachers think the difference in the way students respond to instruction is based on intelligence. It isn't. It's based on filters. When teachers don't know the difference, they blame their students. What complicates this for teachers is that they teach through their own filters.

The following chart shows some typical language and behavior patterns of each.

In Your Experience

Which filter most closely describes you?

_____

OPTION	PROCEDURE
Language - speak in random order, give summaries, use abstract words, not specific	Language - step by step, speak of sequences: first you do so-and-so, use adverbs and adjectives, specify details

Examples:
  big picture
  main idea
  the important thing is
  in general
	Examples:
	  specifically
	  exactly
	  precisely
	  Student indicates: *"I don't understand how to do it."*

Behavior - gets bored when teacher demonstrates the procedure; catches on fast, goes ahead, causes trouble when bored. Can handle some details for short periods Extra work - rewards for something they already like kill motivation. Say: *"All of you who finish within the first twenty min can have some extra FUN by getting some more work from the basket."*	**Behavior** – gets lost and confused when teacher doesn't provide HOW to do a task. Needs written steps with examples. Without steps they become confused and self-distract (talk, throw something, crack a joke, get up and move).

List the names of three students who fit an option filter.

_____

_____

_____

List the names of three students who fit a procedure filter.

_____

_____

_____

The challenge is not to teach through your own filter. A good teacher instructs with both. Here are some helpful strategies.

Chunking Down for Success

Because much of your success depends on whether students get the job done on time, it's important for them to have easy ways to do it. Look at the following groups of letters:

C IAN BCT WAN BAC PR

At first glance they seem difficult to memorize. With simple chunking, look at them now:

CIA NBC TWA NBA CPR

These common acronyms in meaningful chunks are easy to remember.

Older research gave us the 7 ± 2 rule—the brain can hold only seven plus or minus two bits of information at any given time. That's why phone numbers have seven digits, there are seven days of the week, seven continents, etc.

Technology goes even smaller. Newer research says two to four chunks are better. The process of mental organization decrees that the mind can't process content overloaded into a small period.

Organizing Tasks

We talked about how the mind organizes tasks into a hierarchy. Teachers put too much information on the board to save time. This results in the opposite of what you intend.

Too much information trains students' minds to treat data equally. This creates conflict and anxiety; they distract themselves (talk, get up, dig in a backpacks or purse, etc.). You spend precious time in a tug of war to get them back on task. Frustrating.

Avoid this: present information in a way that makes it easy to process. List the tasks in order of importance. Organize the information in bite-sized chunks with no more than three bullets per chunk.

How to Successfully Use the Step Chart

Eighth grade teacher Melvin Phinque was upset: more than 90% of his students failed their history exam. And here's the catch: it was an open book test. How did it happen?

We discovered the students didn't know *how* to take an open book test. He created a Step Chart entitled: *How to Complete an Open Book Test Successfully*.

Step Chart—Completing an Open Book Test Successfully

Step 1: Copy the questions; leave five lines between each question.

Step 2: Find the answers in the book on pages 79 through 97.

Step 3: Write the answers in complete sentences.

Step 4: Find answers by:
    Checking the CHAPTER SUBTITLES
    Checking the INDEX
    Checking the TABLE OF CONTENTS
    Checking YOUR Notes
    Asking a Neighbor

Step 5: When you're done, get an activity out of one of the baskets located in corners of the room and complete it.

He went over it with his students and guess what happened? Test scores skyrocketed. Step Charts are an example of an advanced organizer, which helps students learn better, especially when you include graphics.

Another Success Story

Ms. Eversingle teaches high school math. Although she put time and energy into her lesson, her students didn't get it. During seat work, hands went up all over the room. She found herself teaching the same concepts repeatedly. By the end of the day she was wiped out and the students still didn't learn the material. She decided to put up Step Charts for solving problems.

It worked so well that even when students missed instruction, the Step Chart helped them get through the work fast and easy.

When students ask about a problem or procedure, point to the Step Chart or a rubric. They can compare their work to it and make corrections as needed. It also helps cement learning.

I want you to be curious about something. If you correct their work, who gets additional practice? You do. When your students self-correct, it doubles learning. This works even better when you know how to handle off task behaviors with ease.

When They Go Off Task

Students generally have the attention span of a mosquito. Their minds wander. You must gently bring them back into focus. One effective way is a time call ("Three minutes---two minutes---one minute---)

This works because we are in one of three moods at any given time: cooperative, resistant, or pleasure seeking. Your words put your students in either a cooperative or a resistant mood.

Students in pleasure mode need time.

True story: David was late to school almost every day. During a parent-teacher conference his mom complained that waking him up each morning took over half an hour and left him in a foul mood. I suggested go into his room ten minutes before she wanted him to waken and say, "David, you have rested long enough. You will wake up in ten minutes feeling refreshed and happy." She tried it the next morning. David arrived at school on time for the first time in three months. His mother said he woke up *by himself* in a pleasant mood.

This principle works the same way in your classroom. Give students time to get back on task.

DISARMING RESISTANCE

When someone is is resistant mode you have to do something to put him in a cooperative mode. Use Influential Language: (disarms resistance). Example: You've asked Judith Jumpleski to sit down and she states she doesn't feel like it.

- *I understand* you don't feel like sitting down, but it's important for you to sit down now

- *I know what you mean* but it's important for you to sit down now

- *Thank you for sharing that.* Sit down now.

HOW TO EASILY APPLY IT

1. Chunk down larger assignments and set a time limit.

2. Put no more than three ideas or chunks of information on the board at a time. Use tape to create sections and color coding, making it easier to understand. ALWAYS list brief, specific directions.

3. Use Step Charts and rubrics to clearly outline your expectations, even for behavior. Never assume they know how to do what you want. Program cooperation in their muscle memory. Chapter Twelve will explain this.

4. Require students to have 100% Self-Correcting Mastery; correcting mistakes cements learning.

5. Disarm resistance with Influential Language.

CHAPTER ELEVEN

The Secret of Successful Communication

"THE DIFFERENCE BETWEEN THE RIGHT
WORD AND THE ALMOST RIGHT WORD IS THE
DIFFERENCE BETWEEN LIGHTNING AND A
LIGHTNING BUG"
—*Twain (Mark, Not Shania)*

In a training session I remarked, "The purpose of communication is to get what we want." A principal responded, "Well, I don't always want something when I'm talking to someone."

"Really?"

She thought about it a moment and said, "Actually you're right. We are trying to get something when we talk to someone."

Too many of us are not good at getting responses we want, and too many of us are unskilled in receiving them. Words and actions elicit results. Observe each response and determine if what you get is the one you want. This chapter will help you develop more skill in this area. A wise man said, "If you always do what you have always done, you will always get what you have always gotten."

To get what you want is to know what it is and communicate in a way people understand. You can judge that understanding by their responses. This chapter explains the nitty gritty of communication. I heard a genius say, "It's not what you said, it's what they heard."

In this chapter you will discover:

- Whether your communication style is indirect or direct

- Mistakes to avoid

- How to gain more respect and appreciation from students and parents

- How to come across as meaning business

Is Your Communication Style Direct or Indirect?

Several students were talking in the back of a classroom. The teacher said, "Hey, I'm trying to teach here." The kids ignored her and continued to talk.

Why? Some people talk indirectly. Their meaning is conveyed by suggestion or implication. This might work with adults, but not with students (or men). They see indirect communication not as an order or request but as information.

The teacher wanted the students to be quiet and focus. Instead of saying so, she naively assumed hinting would help. Speaking indirectly leaves it to the student to decipher what you mean and what you want. He may not be able or willing to do so. If the teacher says, "I can't hear myself think," students will ignore her and keep talking.

Have you ever said something in hopes a third person (for whom the message was intended) would get it? That's also indirect communication, which children (and men) unfortunately don't understand. Brief, short injunctions work best for children. Why?

Emotion comes from the subconscious. Children's emotions are up front; your words go directly to their subconscious mind and influence their feelings and behavior.

Mistakes to Avoid

1. Communicating without knowing what you want. Before any interaction, decide what response you want and ask for it.

2. Assuming others know what you want. This is one of the main causes of conflict in relationships. Women are notorious for thinking others (mainly men) can read their minds. Your students can't read your mind. (Which is probably a good thing considering you've got a Chippendale calendar on your computer.) Even when you tell students what you want, they might not understand; *meaning is in people not in words. Make your meaning clear.*

3. Assuming you know what others' words mean. Dr. K. S. Wiggins, social psychologist, says, "Ninety percent of all conflict stems from a problem with definitions."

4. People speak in abstract terms. Assuming you know what their words mean causes conflict. You have a relationship with everyone in your classroom. Important relationship words (such as respect, appreciation, understanding) are nominalizations (anything you can't see on the back of a truck). If you assume you know what they mean, you're setting yourself up for a major misunderstanding.

5. A more effective approach is to ask. Example: a student says, "He disrespected me." ASK:

   Who disrespected you?

   How specifically did he disrespect you?

The meaning of certain words is instilled from birth to age four (even up to age seven). Experiences in the home during this formative period determine verbal understanding.

Understand how your students relate to meanings. This may be different from your experience with the same words. Make sure they know exactly what you mean when you use relationship words.

Get More Respect and Appreciation from Your Students

You want more respect from students and parents. Ask yourself questions to discover what respect means to you. Pay attention to your answers. Remember to ask yourself at least three times.

- *How will I know when this person respects me?*
- *What else will let me know when this person respects me?*
- *What three things can he do to make me feel respected?*

The answers determine what you ask for. You might say, "You know, Mrs. Entwhistle, I feel respected when you get Hobart to do his homework," Consistent practice of this technique will make it natural to you.

Come Across as Meaning Business

A couple in a movie scene sat in an upscale, candlelit restaurant. She looked longingly into his eyes and said, "I am so happy to be with you." Her head slowly shook from side to side.

"Right or wrong, the receiver of the communication tends to base the intentions of the sender on the nonverbal cues he receives." (Website; Nonverbal Communication) Unfortunately people say yes while they nod no, a subconscious reaction. The listener will go with the nonverbal. Research confirms that 93% of messages are communicated without words, and students invariably follow what we do. If you say STOP and your behavior indicates GO, students will go with the GO.

Example: A teacher circulated, helping her students. After three of them asked about the same problem, the teacher knew it was time for some re-teaching. She walked to the board, saying "Okay class, stop working and look at me." The students looked up, saw her walking, and continued to work, eyes down.

By the time she got to the front of the room she had lost them. She scolded, "I said stop working and look at me," not knowing they had already done so. Her movement prompted them to continue studying.

A more effective approach is to walk to the front of the room, stand still, and ask for their attention. Her mouth and body language confirm the message: stop and pay attention.

HOW TO EASILY APPLY IT

1. Speak directly to children.

2. Tell them *exactly* what you want. Make it short, sweet, and to the point.

3. Never depend on students to decipher what you mean. Make your meaning clear.

4. Know what you want BEFORE entering into a conversation. Ask for it. Never assume others know what you want.

5. Never assume you know what others' words mean. Get clarification.

6. Make sure your nonverbal matches your verbal.

CHAPTER TWELVE

Program Cooperation into Muscle Memory

"THE MORE WORDS YOU USE, THE LESS POWER
YOU HAVE."
—*Jackson [not the Five]*

Teachers have a mental image of how teachers should behave and how students should behave. Students have a mental image of how teachers should behave and how students should behave. If the programs match you have harmony. If not you have conflict.

In this chapter you will discover:

- How to make teacher-student programs match
- Emotionally Competent ways to enforce rules
- How Procedure Practice helps

Make Sure Teacher-Student Programs Match

Okay, we know rules are important. Even students know it. So why is cooperation such a struggle? Several reasons: Students don't understand exactly what your rules are. They take enforcement personally. They don't see rules as beneficial.

Arguing and threatening make things worse. Perception of an experience as threatening sends the brain into low gear—a narrowing of understanding that inhibits cognitive functioning. How do you get rid of the painful tug of war with rules? The first step is to make sure you are understood.

What Does "Understand" Really Mean?

Nobody can give you what you want unless he understands what it is. To understand is to process consciously and subconsciously. Example: a dominant visual will process in his conscious system (visual) and in one of the unconscious systems (auditory or kinesthetic).

Teach by showing, telling, and demonstrating the rules. Be sensory specific. Example: "Be nice" is too general. Demonstrate: *What does nice look like? What does it sound like? What kinds of actions are 'nice'?* Have students role play the rules. Have them practice getting it right. These powerful methods program cooperation into muscle memory.

One of the rules on a classroom wall stated "Be respectful." Under that was the question *What does 'respect' look, sound, and feel like in our classroom?* Students had drawn, cut out, and pasted pictures to show respect. One picture showed students raising their hands. In another, the teacher talked and students listened. One showed two students calmly discussing conflict solution.

Emotionally Competent Ways to Enforce Rules

A teacher complained that some of her students seemed to forget the rules. She found herself reminding them repeatedly. Still they resisted. Some even accused her of picking on them.

Remember you are dealing with immature minds swimming in emotion. Feelings rule. Sometimes the message drowns in the emotion. Students react in anger, mistaking themselves for the issue. This is an example of what Dr. Pearsall, in his book *The Heart's Code*, describes as "the lower brain taking the higher brain hostage."

Avoid this with Traffic Signals, which remove personal focus and neutralize issues, keeping you both from feeling attacked, manipulated, or embarrassed.

How do city officials manage the behavior of the citizens? Do they stand in a lofty tower and call out commands? No. Trying to manage the behavior of your students verbally is like standing in the middle of the busiest intersection and directing traffic—confusing, frustrating, even dangerous.

These kids have been in school for years, but they haven't been in your classroom until now. Use a Traffic Signal to show the appropriate way to carry out *your* expectations and procedures.

The Traffic Signal

- Tells, shows (uses graphics), and demonstrates what you expect

- Eliminates misunderstanding—it is very specific

- Eliminates the "help me, help me . . . I don't know what to do" syndrome and helps students become self-directed and autonomous

Post it and point when needed. The sign enforces the expectation. Here are a few examples.

Electronics away.

Bathroom Policy
(The 15 Minute Rule)

1. The first and last fifteen minutes of class, no bathroom.

2. Emergency use allowed during the middle 20 minutes of class.

3. If you go, **you pay back** two minutes at the end of the period.

(Delightfully, I have a book of ready-made signs for you. You can go to www.superachievement.net/trafficsignals and own your FREE copy now).

The Easiest Way to Use Procedure Practice

In high stress situations, the mind is concerned only with safety. The fight, freeze, or flight mechanism kicks in. Without direction, people will do what *they* think is best at the time, adding fuel to the flame. Practicing what to do (fire drills, etc) keeps things running as smoothly as possible and helps people feel safe.

Procedure Practice helps you manage the classroom efficiently. It programs cooperation into muscle memory (the muscles in your body behave automatically). Examples: sitting, standing, talking, which have become routine through experience. Procedure Practice accomplishes the same thing.

When students consistently practice skills and expectations until they get them right, they achieve success. Tell them you want them to be successful and happy this year. And it's important to practice so they can become success masters.

Practicing a skill a few minutes before a desired activity (recess, lunch, games) ensures compliance with speed and ease. It works even better when you say: *We'll enjoy our recess as soon as we succeed.*

This promotes cooperation in the event of pending disaster (like a sub taking over in your absence or you having a breakdown right there in the classroom). Management will become easy during high stress times like testing, extreme weather, or when you're feeling more depressed than usual. It helps prepare students to be successful in the real world.

Use this innovative strategy to get your students to deftly:

- Take out books and materials
- Pass in papers

- Put trash where it belongs
- Walk confidently in the hallways
- Conquer the physiology of paying attention: *show me what it looks like, what it sounds like. What's your body position when you're paying attention?*

The lesson: Our teacher cares enough to help us be successful.

HOW TO EASILY APPLY IT

1. Make a Traffic Signal for rules and procedures. The more graphics, the better. Keep words specific and brief.
2. Post and point when needed.
3. Unwanted behavior signifies misunderstanding. Have students practice skills and expectations until they succeed.

CHAPTER THIRTEEN

How to Create a Safe Classroom Environment

"LEARNING FAILURE RESULTS WHEN THREAT
SHUTS DOWN THE BRAIN.
—Leslie Hart

Students have a fundamental need to know school is physically and emotionally safe. Without that feeling of safety, the rest is a waste of time.

People who fear for their safety go into protective mode. They fight, flee, or freeze. What if there was a way to get students to help you establish and maintain a safe school?

In this chapter, you will discover:

- Subconscious drivers

- Two easy questions that put students in a cooperative mood

- How to respond effectively to anger, rudeness, rebellion, defiance, fear, and restlessness

- How to diffuse hotheads

- How to create and maintain a healthy and happy school climate

Understanding Subconscious Drivers

People do what they do subconsciously. Here's how it works:

(1) Under normal circumstances, your conscious mind is forward. Guilt, fear, anger, anxiety, and stress impel the subconscious forward, absorbing and processing sensory input. You accept suggestions that match your state of mind.

Example: if a child feels angry or bored and you say, "What's wrong with you? You are always fooling around," you just planted two very powerful beliefs: *something is wrong with you; you're always fooling around.* You can be sure painful behavior will follow.

Children's emotions are already dominant, so everything goes directly into the subconscious and influences behavior; creates beliefs about themselves and their ability to learn; creates and affects their self-talk (*what's wrong with me? How come I can't learn? Am I dumb?*).

(2) Repetition—anything you've been exposed to a certain number of times (usually three) bypasses the critical factor and goes directly into your subconscious. Example: if a child has been told "you're a slow learner" over and over, that harmful belief is in his inner mind, influencing his behavior. He'll say things like "It's hard! I can't do it. It's no use." He shuts down when confronted with challenges.

(3) People make mistakes through fear of rejection and abandonment. Both fears are connected to the strong need to belong and render you susceptible to fashion trends and groupthink. What a certain number of people believe, you start to believe too. This explains why kids go along with the obnoxious and annoying behavior of classmates.

Since the root of these problems is at the subconscious level, the solution needs to be there. The next few sections will help.

Two Easy Questions that Put Students in a Cooperative Mood

Have you ever heard a song that reminded you of a pleasant past experience? You picture and relive that experience. You hear sounds and voices. You feel what you felt. The song triggered a happy reaction and put you in a pleasurable state.

Tastes and *smells* bring to memory experiences and trigger reactions. Studies show that the sense of smell elicits a strong response and is a powerful tool for putting people into specific states, which helps explain why overpriced scented candles and essence oils sell so well.

Memories are coded within our five senses. Because of that we say and do things that cause others to relive the past—see the sights, hear the sounds, experience the emotion.

Most of your students have experienced a happy, confident, or cooperative state of mind. These resourceful states make it easy to get the positive behavior that helps us move closer to our goals. Anxiety, fear, and anger generate behavior that works against us.

What makes that significant? Since the students in your classroom have already experienced a learning state, you can do and say things to put them into that or any other state with speed and ease.

Remember that people do what they do because of how they feel. If you want your students to comply, make them feel good about it.

Use questioning strategy. Remember, a question about a past experience forces you to re-experience it consciously and subconsciously. The right question will cause the listener to experience the mood you have asked about. Any of the following will put a student in a cooperative mood:

- *Are you ready to cooperate?*
- *How do you know when you're ready to cooperate?*
- *How will you feel when you cooperate?*

Occasionally the above questions are difficult to answer. If so, create a specific context. Ask: *When was the last time you felt really cooperative?*

An Important Point

How you ask questions is vitally important. Ask as if you are experiencing the mood in question. If you ask *"When was the last time you felt happy?"* with a flat voice and a frown, you will not create a happy mood.

Speak and look as if you are experiencing a productive mood when you ask a question geared to invoke a productive response. Why is this important?

Messages are picked up subconsciously. Remember, when messages are not in sync, the listener will go with the non-verbal.

In Your Experience

Example #1—Mrs. Goodbody's students have been working for five minutes. David hasn't started. She walks over and says, "David, you don't seem to be your normal productive self today, getting things done." He responds, "I just don't feel like it. I got a lot on my mind." Mrs. Goodbody decides to use the powerful Questioning Strategy.

Write two questions that will put David in a productive mood.

a. _____

b. _____

Example #2—Mr. Throgbottom's students plan to work with partners on an assignment. He remembers what happened the last time he assigned Treniese to work with Griselda. Treniese angrily demanded, "Why do I have to work with her?" Mr. T decides to use the Questioning Strategy to put the class in a cooperative mood *before* assigning partners. What questions can he ask?

a. _____

b. _____

Rudeness, Rebellion, Defiance, and Restlessness

The biggest cause of misbehavior is negative feeling. People interpret what is happening to them based on their environment. Example: a teacher asked a student to give her his cell phone. The boy refused. In the boy's environment, handing over your phone meant losing it. The teacher promised, "I will hold your phone until the end of school. Then you'll get it back." The boy complied.

Another cause of misbehavior is conditioning. Some boys have been programmed to say no to women. They need time to process the directions of a female teacher. Teachers demand immediacy. Not understanding, teachers react to the above situations by sending these negatively programmed boys to the office. I understand why you may have done so in the past, but here's a better solution.

Subconscious Friendly Ways for Handling:

1. Rebellion. Teach negotiation: students need to know rebellion against authority is a losing game. Teachers have the power to suspend or expel defiant students. This is the purpose of communication skills: your students need to know how to negotiate a win-win in the classroom.

   Negotiation and compromise are a large part of healthy assertive communication. This takes place when both parties in a conversation are willing to ask:

- *What do you want and how can we work together to get it?*
- *Here's what I want, how can we negotiate so that we're both happy?*
- *We seem to want different things here; what can we do to get both of us most of what we want?*

  In order to get along in the world and be happy, you have to defer to people in authority over you: teachers, bosses, parents, drill sergeants, probation officers, the IRS, you get the idea.

  Students need to make a distinction between *wanting to* and *being willing* to. Example: the teacher expects students to complete and turn in homework. Students don't want to but must be willing if they desire future happiness and a place in the world.

- Defiance: use the STOP-START Formula (gain immediate compliance). When you want them to **stop** doing something, replace it with a **start** of something else because the mind doesn't like an empty space-- it will fill it. Examples:

  Stop arguing and sit down now.

  Stop talking and pay attention now.

  Continue sitting there and start working now.

  Why does this work? The subconscious doesn't know which command to follow, so it does both.

2. Rudeness: Never tolerate it. Use the STOP-START Formula: *Never use foul language in this classroom. Use only respectful words in this classroom.* (This works even better when you have a list of those respectful words posted.)

3. Fear: "What are you afraid might happen?" After a student expresses fear, say: "Stop feeling that way. Go to a better feeling now."

NOTE: Protect your student: If there is real danger, report it to proper authorities.

4. Restlessness: find the cause: *And you're restless because...* The student is likely bored or confused.

    Boredom = teacher hasn't explained "What's in it for me?"

    Confusion = teacher needs to explain assignments clearly

You can sidestep many issues by teaching students how to use language to solve conflicts and get what they want. The ability to handle emotion foretells academic success. Students who effectively manage emotion become more resilient against failure.

The last decade has seen an alarming rise in school violence. That violence is often the result of frustration. When a student lacks coping skills and feels he has no other options, his chances of responding with violence drastically increase.

Hidden Causes of Violence

(1) We not only have feelings, we have feelings about those feelings. If we are angry, we are angry about feeling angry (*why do I have to feel this way?*), which triggers violence.

(2) Models teach us to behave with violence. Children witness domestic and neighborhood violence. In movies and on TV, even heroes react to displeasure with violence.

(3) Violence stems from fear. People who fear being attacked attack first. The mind tells them their actions are self-protective. On his first day, a student hit several children and called them names. Questioning revealed that in his old school he was bullied. Afraid others would pick on him here, he lashed out.

Understanding these causes is the first step to finding solutions: it is imperative that we teach students the function of anger and how to express it in a non-violent way. It is vital to expose violent models as wrong and teach children verbal skills for handling conflict.

By reframing fear and helping young people find appropriate ways to protect themselves, we equip them with skills that render them able to diffuse and avoid unhealthy conflict.

Diffusing Hotheads

Have you ever dealt with angry parents? Silly question, of course you have. You are probably still traumatized by the yelling, swearing, hair pulling, and general threats you have been forced (sometimes on your own time) to put up with. What can you do?

Decide your desired results.

(1) Diffuse anger first. Try this: *Thank you for calming down.* This works because your conscious mind is out front. When anger is present, the subconscious mind takes over. Your words go straight to the subconscious and influence behavior.

(2) If (1) doesn't work, state what is occurring and add a direction. Example: *You're screaming and cursing. Thank you for lowering your voice and for not cursing.*

You eliminate angry outbursts for good when you remove the root cause. This requires knowing why parents are angry and eliminating the source of the anger.

Create and Maintain a Positive Climate

A middle school teacher admitted he did not like his ill-behaved students. If you don't like your students they will know it from your verbal and nonverbal clues.

In alternative education, I taught students kicked out of regular school for nightmarish behaviors. My kids consisted of "gangbangers," students on probation, etc. They came to me unmotivated, hating school, feeling trapped. I had very high expectations, tolerated no nonsense, and insisted they learn. Even when I gave well-deserved F minuses, I was voted most popular teacher. When I asked why, they told me, "We know you love us. All of us felt you wanted our highest good."

Do you want to see students do well not only academically but in life? If you don't teach with this degree of devotion, your students will pick up on it. You are destined to fail.

Every School Has Its Own Climate

"When the emotional atmosphere is calm and positive, problems that could be potentially lethal are often handled very objectively." (Friedman)

When I hear of angry outbursts and management problems I know it's time to check the climate.

In one school teachers regarded the students as the enemy and vice versa. That signaled an "against" climate, one that states "I don't want to be here." And if students don't want to be there, teachers don't want them there either.

Another climate destroyer is friction between teachers. I visited a school where teachers habitually badmouthed each other. A rift existed between principal and staff. There were union threats. The kids were bouncing off the walls. The parents threatened legal action. No one felt safe.

Climate is created subconsciously, its painful results overtly manifested. Low test scores, fights, high suspension rates, and more. Parents flee; you don't get the respect you deserve as a teacher. Find out what is sabotaging your climate and change it.

Any of these questions will uncover your secret school climate:

- *What message do you get from this school?*
- *How do you feel about this school?*
- *If you could, what would you change?*

OPTIMIZING YOUR CLIMATE
(Seeks what is in the BEST INTEREST for all)

EU Sabotagers

Uses FORCE - (language: should, have to, must, ought to)

+ Criticism, judgment, blaming
+ Ignoring conflict
+ Using fear or threats (screaming)
+ Negative interpretation of events

AGAINST **MINDSET: US vs. THEM**
I don't want to be here. I don't like them.
They are the enemy. What's wrong with them?

**Results in angry outbursts, fights, cursing, noncompliance,
achievement gaps**

EU Lifelines

Empowers - (language: choose, decide, allow, it's best)

+ Forgiveness, understanding, acceptance
+ Finding the BEST options for solving conflict
+ Using (positive) questions to optimize performance
+ Chooses the best in every circumstance

FOR **MINDSET: We have your best interest at heart**
How can we make the most of this situation?
How can we bring out the best in others?
How can I be my best self in this?

Results in happier teaching and learning, better behavior, and
higher achievement.

Behavior is determined by EU

Emotional Undercurrent
Are they FOR us or AGAINST us?
(CLIMATE)

IMPORTANT NOTE

Ask these questions of an outsider who can objectively evaluate your situation. When a question is not responded to well, ask another. And avoid doing this kind of research in a survey. A survey requires thought, and when you think, your brain lights up as if you put your hand in ice water. Painful. People don't like to think and won't respond well to the survey.

These powerful questions are best answered face-to-face. This compels the respondent to think, taps his need for approval, and gets you the answers you need.

Asking "What do you like least about this place?" is confrontational. Ask a benign question first. Soften it with *What do you like most about this school?* If there is a problem, you'll be told about it. You may not even need to ask the "least" question.

HOW TO EASILY APPLY IT

1. Understand that people do what they do subconsciously. Children's emotions are already prevalent so watch what you say. Speak as positively as possible.

2. Gain pleasant cooperation by putting students into a cooperative state of mind. A question is your most powerful tool.

3. Diffuse angry parents or other adults. If you want them to be calm, thank them for being calm.

4. Create and maintain a positive, safe classroom environment.

6. If there are angry outbursts, fights, and conflicts on your campus, your climate is suspect. Find out what is sabotaging that climate and change it.

7. Always teach your children to express how they feel and ask for what they want. This creates a healthy atmosphere and promotes emotional freedom.

EMOTIONAL COMPETENCE

Your Powerful Influence Really Matters

"THE SINGLE MOST IMPORTANT FACTOR IN
PREDICTING STUDENT SUCCESS IS TEACHER
INFLUENCE."
—*Eklund*

She was sweet and funny, but kind of tough.

She let me know when enough was enough.

She took the time to encourage me

to be whatever I wanted to be.

And even when my mother died,

she lent an ear; with me she cried.

I learned I could do anything.

She even let me act and sing.

She taught me things about myself;

the definition of true wealth.

The place in me where none could reach

she touched. Because of her I teach.

*~Written and dedicated by Selina Jackson to
good teachers who care enough.*

My tenth grade year was excruciating: my mother died. Formerly an excellent student, I began showing up in geometry class with a deck of cards in one pocket and a pair of dice in the other. I'd saunter in late, choose my seat at the very back table, and set up my own little Vegas.

I invited other bored, disengaged class members to come lose their money to me. The teacher was furious. He'd storm back to the table, yell and threaten "If you don't like me and if you don't like my class, I'll send you to the dean, you can talk to Mr. Douglas, and you can GET OUT!" He always screamed these last words with great enthusiasm.

I'd look up at him, shake my head and laugh. I told him if he didn't give me a B, I was going to kick his butt. Guess what? He gave me a B. He let me slide. This and other "get away with it" episodes taught me to manipulate teachers by playing the victim, which caused me huge pain in my adult life. I became a financial loser, a doormat in relationships, a victim in every facet of my life. That's what happens when a teacher deals you a pity card.

I regarded one adult in that school differently. She was my history teacher. Miss Bullen demanded respect. She never yelled. She made her expectations very clear and insisted that we carry them out. We did.

She didn't pity me because my mom died and I was bounced from foster home to foster home. Unlike other teachers, she didn't accept my excuses. She demanded a great deal from me and called on me to be my best self. She inspired me to reach past darkness into day.

Do it Even if You Don't Plan to

Your words influence your students. Your actions affect their lives. Inspire them to believe in themselves. You can make them feel sorry for their circumstances or you can encourage them to create better ones.

When you feel good about teaching, it shines through. Inspire your students to feel good about learning and better about themselves.

In Your Experience

1. What is your core purpose? What do you want children to learn, know, experience as a result of your teaching?

_____

_____

_____

2. Why is this important?

_____

_____

_____

3. What makes the things you wrote in number 2 important?

_____

_____

_____

4. What important feeling will you receive from what you wrote in number 3?

_____

_____

_____

5. What's most important to you about helping your students succeed in school and in life?

_____

_____

_____

This book has recalled things you already know, and you have discovered a lot of new information. What's the difference between knowing something and acting on it?

_____

_____

_____

"A TEACHER'S INFLUENCE LIVES ON LONG AFTER THE CAREER IS OVER."
—*Eileen Button*

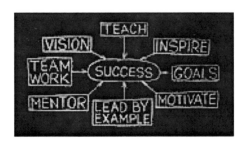

Because of your new understanding, you will become aware that you are automatically using the techniques you've discovered. And your students will surprise you and themselves with how easily and well they learn, leaving you with the deep satisfaction of a job well done.

Success to YOU!

References

INTRODUCTION – EMOTIONAL COMPETENCE: How Teachers Can Get Students to Learn Easier and Faster

1. Hinton C., Miamoto, K., & Della-Chiesa, B. *Brain Research, Learning and Emotions: Implications for education research, policy and practice1. European Journal of Education, Vol. 43, No. 1, 2008*

CHAPTER ONE - Emotional Competence is Important

1. Cooper, R. K., PhD., Sawaf, A. *Executive EQ.* NY: Grosset/ Putnam 1997, pp xii-xiii

2. Restack, R. MD., *The New Brain*, PA: Rodale. pp 36-38. 2003

3. Rosenberg, M., Ph.D. *Nonviolent Communication: A Language of Life*. Puddle Dancer Press, Encinitas, Ca, 2005

4. Hawkins, David. Ph.D. *When Pleasing Others is Hurting You: Finding God's Patterns for Healthy Relationships*. Harvest House Publishers, Eugene, Ore. www.harvesthousepublishers. com. p. 113 2004.

5. ibid. p. 39

6. ibid. p. 156

7. Lazarus, R., *Progress on a Cognitive-Motivational-Relationsal Theory of Emotion*. American Psychology #46, p.827. 1991.

8. Jenson, E., *Ten Most Effective Tips for Using Brain Based Teaching and Learning*. Citations: Koomen, H. M. & Hoeksma, J. B. (2003, Dec). Regulation of emotional security by children after entry to special and regular kindergarten classes. Psychological Reports, 93(3Pt 2):1319-34.

CHAPTER TWO – Designing Your Day for Happier Results

1. Locke, E., Latham, G., *Building a Practicality Useful Theory of Goal Setting and Task Motivation: A 35 Year Oddessy*. American Psychology 579, pp. 705-717. 2002.

2. Latham, G.P., Yuki, G. *A Review of Research on the Applications of Goal Setting in Organizations*, Academy of Management Journal. 1975. pp. 824-845.

3. Ellis, A, Ph.D., Harper, R., Ph.D. *A Guide to Rational Living*. Melvin Powers Wilshire Book Company, Chatsworth, Ca. p. 155. 1997

CHAPTER THREE – The Power of Your Words

1. Amen, Daniel G., MD. *Change Your Brain Change Your Life*. NY: Times Books, 1998, pp 56-60

2. Restak, R.M., *The Brain Has a Mind of It's Own*. New York: Harmony. 1991

3. Seligman, M., *Learned Optimism*, New York: Knopf. 1991 .

PART TWO - The Role of Emotion in Learning

1. Restak, Richard, MD. *Mozart's Brain and the Fighter Pilot*. NY: Harmony Books, 2001, pp 115-116

2. Pert, Candace, PhD. *Molecules of Emotion*. NY: Scribner, 1997, pp 146-147

CHAPTER SIX - Easy Ways to Change Negative Feelings about Learning

1. Patterson, K., Grenny, J., Maxfield, D., McMillan, R., Switzler, A., *Influencer: The Power to Change Anything.* McGraw-Hill, New York. 2008).

2. Rosenthal, R., Jacobson, L. *Pygmalion in the Classroom.* Austin: Holt Rinehart, and Winston 1968

CHAPTER SEVEN - How to Apply the Four Universal Life Motivators to the Classroom

1. Grinder, John & Richard Bandler (1975). *The Structure of Magic II: A Book About Communication and Change*, Palo Alto, CA: Science & Behavior Books.

2. Patterson, K., Grenny, J., Maxfield, D., McMillan, R., Switzler, A., *Influencer: the Power to Change Anything.* McGraw-Hill, New York. p 93. 2008.

CHAPTER EIGHT – Closing the Gap: Easy Ways for Increasing Achievement Among Blacks and Latinos

1. Bandler, Richard; John (1976). *The Structure of Magic II.* Science and behavior Books Inc. p. 7.

2. Gurian, M. *Boys and Girls Learn Differently.* P 190-192. CA: Jossey-Bass, 2001.

3. Herrmann, Ned. *The Whole Brain Business Book.* P 38-41. NY:McGraw-Hill, 1996.

CHAPTER NINE - Strategies for Instant Learning

1. Ibid.

2. Bransford, J. D., Brown, A. L., & Cocking, R. R. (Eds.). *How People Learn: Brain, Mind, Experience, and School.* Washington, DC: National Research Council. 2000.

CHAPTER ELEVEN - The Secret of Successful Communication

1. Website; *Nonverbal Communication*

CHAPTER TWELVE - How to Program Cooperation into their Muscle Memory

1. Pearsall, Paul, PhD. *The Heart's Code*. NY: Broadway Books, 1998, pp 26-27

CHAPTER THIRTEEN - How to Create a Safe Classroom Environment

1. Hart, Leslie A. *Human Brain and Human Learning*. NY: Longman Inc., 1983, pp 108-110

2. Friedman, Edwin H. *Generation to Generation*. NY: The Guilford Press, 1985, pp 240-242

CONCLUSION - Your Powerful Influence Really Matters

1. Eeklund, N., M.Ed. *How Was Your Day at School?: Improving Dialogue about Teacher Job Satisfaction*. Search Institute. 2008.

Index

Symbols

100% Self-Correcting Mastery 111

A

abstract terms 115
achievement 69, 97
advanced organizer 109
amygdala 60
anger 11, 20, 21, 22, 30, 31, 120, 125, 126, 127, 132
angry outbursts 69, 132, 133, 136
anxiety 29, 109, 126
Applying Trigger Statements 78
attention 21, 39, 40, 61, 78, 88, 99, 101, 116, 117, 123
attitude facilitates learning 63
auditory 84, 89, 120

B

behavior 21, 28, 35, 42, 60, 69, 72, 84, 88, 106, 114, 116, 121, 123, 126, 127, 132, 143
behavior patterns 106
beliefs 10, 16, 17, 28, 29, 30, 32, 59, 60, 64, 71, 73, 126
belief system 16, 29, 70
body language 117
boredom 10, 96, 97
brain 30, 35, 36, 91, 95, 98, 108, 120, 125, 135
Brain Filters 11, 106

C

CANCEL factor 72
chunking 108
classroom management 14
climate 11, 126, 133, 136
cognitive filters 105
communicate 88, 89, 114
communication 10, 11, 84, 90, 99, 113, 114, 116

communication filters 90
confidence 27, 93
conflict 16, 20, 46, 88, 89, 109, 115, 119, 120, 132
conflicts 131, 136
Conscious Competence 97
Conscious Incompetence 97
conscious mind 16, 126, 132
conscious system 89, 120
constant and never ending improvement 42, 71
control 31, 34, 35, 41, 44, 105
cooperation 5, 136
coping skills 131
core purpose 139
core values 9, 45
Counteract Other Peoples' Negativity 9, 39
critical factor 29, 126
critical thinking 102
cross-communication 10, 84

D

day-to-day transactions 34
defiance 11, 84, 125
direct communication 11, 28, 29, 114
discipline 33, 84
distracting behaviors 68
distractions 35
diversity 91

E

effort 75
emotion 16, 19, 30, 59, 120, 127
emotional atmosphere 133
Emotional Competence 4, 14, 19, 141
emotional freedom 49
Emotionally Competent 11, 119, 120
emotional messages 21
Emotional Messaging System 9, 20
emotional state 41

emotional system 16
emotional upheaval 30, 55
emotional wealth 54
energy 35, 36, 43, 98, 99, 110
enhance comprehension and retention 10, 96
environment 10, 75, 81, 96, 136
equity 97
ethnic intolerance 90
expectations 69, 70, 92, 93, 111, 121, 122, 123, 133, 138
extroverts 98

F

failure 29, 81, 125, 131
fear 11, 71, 72, 95, 96, 105, 125, 126, 127, 131, 132
feelings 7, 10, 21, 22, 35, 59, 70, 96, 114, 129, 131
female 93
fight, freeze, or flight mechanism 122
fights 133, 136
Finding the Best Solutions to Everyday Challenges 55
focus 35, 41, 68, 85, 90, 110, 114, 121
Four Learning Stages 96
four universal life motivators 10, 76
frame of mind 31, 61
frontal lobe 30
frustration 20, 21, 30, 31
fun 40, 103, 105

G

gestures and body coding 91
goal 20, 21, 34, 35, 46
goals 9, 16, 19, 29, 35, 37, 41, 42, 45, 46, 78, 79, 82, 127
gratitude 54

H

health issues 22
health problems 40
hierarchy of importance 34, 108
high expectations 70, 93, 133

I

indirect communication 11, 114
influence 43, 69, 72, 114, 132, 137, 138, 140
injunctions 114
inspire kids 10, 64
instruction 14, 72, 78, 81, 106, 110
interactive lessons 99
introverts 98

K

kinesthetic 85, 120

L

lack of comprehension 85
language 64, 81, 88, 89, 91, 92, 106, 117, 131
language patterns 106
Latinos 83, 85, 143
Law of Expectation 70
Law of Suggestion 9, 39, 40, 44
learning 5, 10, 33, 35, 41, 42, 59, 60, 61, 63, 64, 65, 66, 71, 73, 77, 79, 81, 82, 83, 84, 95, 96, 97, 99, 100, 101, 110, 111, 127, 139
life purpose 46
limbic system 30, 41
limiting beliefs 30, 32, 60, 73
limiting emotions 17
limiting language 81
love 7, 15, 57, 58, 59, 64, 101, 133

M

managing subconscious priorities 33
Maximizing Your Emotional Competence 53
meaning 11, 40, 60, 98, 99, 114, 115, 117
Meaning Of Your Emotions 20
mental image 119
mental states 19
messages picked up subconsciously 20, 21, 60, 72, 116
messaging system 20

CPSIA information can be obtained at www.ICGtesting.com
Printed in the USA
LVOW06s2040261213

366959LV00003B/4/P

9 780989 232524